THE MILK OF LIONS

The Milk of Lions

A History of Alcohol in the Middle East

by
Joseph El-Asmar

GILGAMESH

THE MILK OF LIONS
A History of Alcohol in the Middle East

Published by Gilgamesh Publishing in 2020
Email: info@gilgamesh-publishing.co.uk
www.gilgamesh-publishing.co.uk

ISBN 978-1-908531-93-3

© Joseph El-Asmar 2020

Note: An Arabic edition of this book was published in Lebanon in 2014.

Acknowledgements
The Author would like to thank Carole Rizk for her work translating the original Arabic into the first drafts of the English version published here.

Cover design: Areej Mahmoud
Body text design: Martin Humphries
Editorial: Asher Kessler

All rights are reserved. No part of this publication may be reproduced, stored in a retrieval system or transmitted in any form or by any means, electronic, mechanical, photographic or otherwise, without prior permission of the copyright holder

CIP Data: A catalogue for this book is available from the British Library

Dedication

To Zeina, Marwan, Walid and Youmna

Contents

PREFACE
Our story… and our acknowledgements · 11

INTRODUCTION
About this book · 15

CHAPTER I
Historical Background · 19

CHAPTER II
Religious Background · 37

CHAPTER III
Alcohol in the Arab World · 63

CHAPTER IV
Alcohol in Lebanon · 115

Glossary · 171

Bibliography · 173

And in the autumn, when you gather the grapes of your
  vineyards for the winepress,
Say in your heart,
"I too am a vineyard, and my fruit shall be gathered for the
  winepress,
And like new wine I shall be kept in eternal vessels."
And in winter, when you draw the wine, let there be
in your heart a song for each cup;
And let there be in the song a remembrance for the autumn
  days,
and for the vineyard, and for the winepress.

Gibran Khalil Gibran

PREFACE

Our story... and our acknowledgements

This story begins with a family decision to build a house in the middle of a vineyard. The land we chose sat above one of the hills surrounding Jezzine, a town 75km south of Beirut famous for its araq. The tradition in the town and the country as a whole of making araq had been slowly dying. By installing a traditional Lebanese still, called a *karaki*, at the house, we aimed to celebrate the season of araq production and preserve our heritage.

I was very curious about the manufacturing process and started searching for scientific and historic references about the craft in public and private libraries, and in the archives of monasteries. But I was surprised to find an almost complete lack of relevant texts. The only information I could find was that passed along from generation to generation, and even then, the tradition would change according to the story, and the person's mood. The process remained the same, of course, but I wanted to know more about the quality and types of materials that produce the best araq. After all, the details and the attention given to each step are what make all the difference.

My research led me to one key question: who invented araq? This in turn led me to another, altogether larger question: who discovered alcohol? And from there to: where were the first alcoholic drinks found? Each answer would lead to a new question and soon enough I had gathered scientific and historical data that had long been neglected by Arab writers, perhaps for religious reasons. But I could not have done this task alone. I owe a great deal in this quest to my wife Zeina Touma. She was the first person to encourage me, and was both a reader and a critic, often drawing my attention to terms, "too difficult for young people to understand," or sentences, "too complicated from a scientific standpoint." I can only hope that this book has done her justice and is a smooth read that brings joy and entertainment. I hope that it brings the past to life for today's generations, who have been slowly forced to abandon their social heritage.

There are so many stories told about the production of araq, and during my research, I ended up hearing most of them. I therefore needed an independent and scientific source to help me discern fact from fiction. For his contributions to this effort, I have to thank Father Charbel Hajjar who reviewed the texts I provided on alcohol in general, and those specific to araq, and gave them his professional "blessing". Father Charbel is a Basilian Chouerite monk who studied oenology

Our story… and our acknowledgements

in France and returned to Lebanon to manage the assets of the St John Monastery in Khenchara. He was given the 2010 Best Red Wine award at the Horeca culinary exhibition.

As I have already mentioned, the stories I found often diverged and were even contradictory at times, and authentic sources were hard to come by. I would like to thank Dr. Tarif Khalidi, researcher in Arab and Islamic history, for his valuable guidance on research methodology and the verification of sources.

A special thank you is also due to Ahmad Asfahani, a journalist specializing in historical documents, who showed enthusiasm for the project from the very beginning. His support in reading the first chapters of this book, and offering criticism, is highly appreciated and has helped shape the book as you see it today.

A final acknowledgement goes out to all those with whom I shared a glass and a toast. The inspiration comes from there…

Joseph El-Asmar
January 2020

INTRODUCTION

About this book

Every people and every community on earth has customs and traditions it practices spontaneously. We may have little understanding of their origins or how they came to be. But it is these customs and traditions that make each community unique, what binds it to a land and an environment.

The Arab world is no different. However, while Arab communities share countless traditions, their attitudes and opinions tend to diverge when it comes to alcoholic drinks. In some communities, we find very strict religious rules, or fatwas, that prohibit the consumption of alcohol (even though the Qur'an itself only calls for its avoidance). Such countries include Saudi Arabia, where the state draws its power from religion and governs through religious dogma. In other countries, like Lebanon, alcohol is widely available and its consumption is not limited by religious texts or civil laws.

All kinds of alcoholic drinks are produced in Lebanon

but the main spirit manufactured there is araq, a drink once considered to be a staple and an honoured tradition all across the Fertile Crescent. Nonetheless, as conservative religious movements gradually gained influence in the region, the production and consumption of araq became largely limited to Lebanon where the country's diversity and unique social and religious structures were more accommodating. The average individual alcohol consumption in Lebanon stands today at approximately 5 litres per year.

It is important to note, however, that very few of the people who consume alcohol, particularly araq, in the Fertile Crescent are alcoholics. On the contrary, araq - and alcohol in general - are synonymous with joy and pleasure, good food and company. People drink araq and other alcoholic beverages as a reward after a long week, to celebrate special occasions or on holidays. It is a way of honouring guests who are usually offered a generous display of delicious dishes to accompany the drink. Araq, as a national drink, is also a source of pride for many - particularly men - who see it as a way to demonstrate their stamina and strength. Gatherings around araq are gatherings of joy, harmony and familiarity between friends and family.

So how did the story of alcohol begin in the Fertile Crescent, and how did these drinks find their way to the rest of the Arab world? Why did araq become so popular to the point of being favoured over other drinks, especially in Lebanon? To answer these questions, we must look into the history of alcoholic drinks. What is the story behind these drinks that can cloud the mind, if only for a brief moment, and allow it to be absorbed by the surrounding mood, place, or environment?

Alcohol has been around for almost as long as man has. This book tells the story of alcoholic drinks across the ages and follows the communities that have adopted them as part of their national identities. It explores the various cultural and religious attitudes regarding alcohol, with an emphasis on the production of Lebanon's own national drink, araq.

CHAPTER I

Historical Background

After the Flood

The Beginnings

Beer, from Sumer to Egypt

The Pharoahs and Alcohol

AFTER THE FLOOD

And Noah began to be a husbandman, and he planted a vineyard; And he drank of the wine and was drunken; and he was uncovered within his tent.
(Genesis 9:20-21)

This is one of the oldest written mentions of vineyards, alcohol and drunkenness. Other books of the Bible also mention wine on various occasions.

Noah's first act after stepping foot on dry land was to plant a vineyard, making wine an essential part of man's life on the reborn Earth.

In fact, the Old Testament gives great importance to alcohol, and offers sermons and guidance on drinking. For example, in the Book of Chronicles, priests who drink wine when entering the inner court face death.

… And the Lord spake unto Aaron, saying, Do not drink wine nor strong drink, thou, nor thy sons with thee, when ye go into the tabernacle of the congregation, lest ye die; it shall be a statute forever throughout your generations.
(Leviticus 10:8-9)

In the Book of Judges, the vine was crowned king for giving the gift of wine.

> *Then said the trees unto the vine, Come thou and reign over us,*
> *And the Vine said unto to them,*
> *Should I leave my wine, which cheereth God and man, and go to be promoted over all the trees?*
> (Judges 9:12-13)

In the Psalms, wine is considered a source of joy and happiness:

> *And wine that maketh glad the heart of man, and oil to make his face to shine, and bread which strengtheneth man's heart*
> (Psalm 104: 14-15)

The saying 'a little bit of wine gladdens a man's heart' has even become popular and is often wrongly attributed to Jesus Christ.

The Wisdom of Sirach interestingly starts off by warning of the dangers of wine:

> *Wine and women will make men of understanding to fall away: and he that cleaveth to harlots will become impudent*
> (Sirach 19:2)

Only to conclude by praising it, and setting the rules and principles of drinking:

> *Shew not thy valiantness in wine; for wine hath destroyed many.*
> *The furnace proveth the edge by dipping: so doth wine the hearts of the proud by drunkeness.*
> *Wine is as good as life to a man, if it be drunk moderately: what life is then to a man that is without wine? for it was made to make men glad.*
> *Wine measurably drunk and in season bringeth gladness of the heart, and cheerfulness of the mind:*
> *But wine drunken with excess maketh bitterness of the mind, with brawling and quarrelling.*
> *Drunkenness increaseth the rage of a fool till he offend: it diminisheth strength, and maketh wounds.*
> *Rebuke not thy neighbour at the wine, and despise him not in his mirth: give him no despiteful words, and press not upon him with urging him to drink.*

(Sirach 31:25-31)

This has been the story of wine from the very beginning; rejected by some but bringing joy to others. From the earliest times, people have tried to avoid the bad in alcohol and stick to the good, and provide advice and guidelines on how to drink.

THE BEGINNINGS

The first alcoholic drink man ever drank was beer. In fact, beer is as old as civilization itself. It was one of the first drinks produced when, some time around 10,000 BC to 15,000 BC, communities of hunter-gathers settled and became farmers.

Indeed, some scholars (such as the biomolecular archaeologist, Patrick McGovern) believe that man started making beer even before making bread, while others would argue that bread came first. No one really knows who discovered the fermentation process that led to the drink, but it most likely happened by accident. It is possible, for example, that water got into jars containing leftover bread Left for a while, bubbles formed at the top. People drank the liquid and were amazed by its sweet taste and the joy it brought them. They considered it a gift from the gods.

The oldest evidence discovered of the existence of beer in ancient civilizations is a stone tablet dating back to 6,000 BC that suggests that the Sumerians were the first to discover the fermentation process leading to beer. The Sumerians are the ancient inhabitants of Sumer, the southern part of Mesopotamia, or Iraq as we know it today.

Researchers later discovered a hymn written on cuneiform tablets praising Ninkasi, the Sumerian goddess of beer, and describing the best recipe:

Ninkasi, you hold with both hands the great sweet wort,
Ninkasi, you pour out the filtered beer from the jars,
To flow like the Tigris and the Euphrates.

The Sumerians produced around 20 different types of beer. They drank their beer in jars through a pipe or a reed, in order not to stir the bitter dregs of fermentation at the bottom

Beer also played a significant cultural role for the Sumerians. Perhaps most famously, the barbarian character Enkidu was transformed into a human after eating bread and drinking beer. *The Epic of Gilgamesh*, one of the oldest great works of literature, tells the tale of the fifth king of Sumer, Enkidu, who used to eat grass and drink the milk of animals, and wanted to show off his strength in front of the demi-god, Gilgamesh. Wary, Gilgamesh sent a nymph to find out Enkidu's strengths and weaknesses. Enkidu spent a week of pleasure with the nymph, during which she taught him about the ways of civilized life, and about bread and beer. She said to him, 'Eat the bread, it is the way one lives. Drink the beer, it is the gift of the land.' Enkidu ate and drank seven jugs, and felt his heart be lifted to the skies. He then rubbed his body with oil and became a man. According to Sumerian custom, to eat bread, drink beer and rub oil on a loved one was a confirmation of the strong relationship that binds two people.

The Code of Hammurabi, written in 2100 BC and considered to be the oldest codification of law in the world, sets the daily ration of beer for each member of the community, according to their status, the equivalent of:
- Two litres for workers
- Three litres for servants
- Five litres for officials and priests

The code also imposes harsh penalties on anyone who cheats a fellow man when it comes to beer, whether at home or at a tavern, and on anyone who is seen inebriated. For example, a priest is to be burned to death if witnessed drunk.

Sumer far preferred beer to wine. While beer was so important to the Sumerians that they had a deity of beer, wine production was scarce and drinking wine was limited to the high society. Wine in Sumer was not only made from grapes, but also from dates, figs, or some combination of these fruits. Dates and figs were better suited to cultivation in Sumer given the region's dry and sunny climate. Historical references show that grapes were sometimes imported to Sumer from Turkey, Syria, and Palestine where the soil and environment were far more suited to the cultivation of the vine.

Historical Background

BEER, FROM SUMER TO EGYPT

From Mesopotamia, the next great civilization to discover, and fall in love with beer was the Nubians in Upper Egypt. Around 3,600 BC, Egyptian civilization was prospering on the banks of the Nile and the Egyptians were making beautiful and distinctively decorated pottery similar to what was being made in Palestine. They had borrowed their construction systems and methods from the Sumerians, with arches and arcades prevalent in many structures and reliefs with various dimensions decorating the walls. The use of copper was also widespread at the time. During the same period, around 3,200 BC, Narmer the King of Upper Egypt was leading a movement to unify his kingdom (symbolised by the lotus) with Lower Egypt (symbolised by the papyrus).

Upper Egypt, then known as the Kingdom of Kush, stretched from the north of Egypt to the south of Sudan. The Kingdom even included the city of Khartoum were the Nubians lived around 5,000 years BC and where they established kingdoms whose power reached the Nile valley, Egypt, Palestine and even southern Turkey.

Along with bread, beer was a staple in ancient Egypt. However, the beer they drank every day was not quite the same beer we know today. It was dark, viscous, and contained hard grains. In fact, it most resembles the traditional North African dish known as asida, which is a type of pudding made from wheat flower and yoghurt. Beer was the ancient Egyptians' most important source of protein, minerals, and vitamins and was so important that the jars it was kept in were also used in medicine to measure precious and costly materials.

Not much information is available about the different types of beer they had. Researchers have so far discovered a sweet beer but cannot yet offer many useful details about its composition.

Conical-shaped jars have been discovered in Asyut and Luxor dating back to the pre-pharaonic period in the temples of the cities of Nekhen and Abydos. At the bottom of these jars, traces of corn starch have been found and evidence that the jars were placed over fire. While there is no evidence that they were used for fermentation, scientists can confirm that early versions of beer were made from "beer bread," a type of well-leavened dough that is baked in such a way as to keep some of the yeast active. The mixture was then crumbled over a sieve and left to ferment in jars. There is also no scientific evidence that dates or barley were used to make beer during this period.

After analysing the residue found at the bottom of the discovered jars, researchers were able to discover new fermentation processes. As an alternative to beer bread, the Egyptians would peel the grains to extract the enzymes and cook a similar amount of the grains to get the starch. The two components would then be mixed together to allow the enzymes to interact with the starch and produce the sugar. The skins would then be removed from the resulting mixture, to which yeast would be added to obtain alcohol. This method is still widely used today in some African countries.

Historical Background

The anthropologist Georges Armelagos and his team studied human bones dating back to 350-550 BC discovered in Upper Egypt. They found that the bones contained tetracycline, an antibiotic that is used today to treat acne, urinary tract infections and other illnesses. The first antibiotic to be discovered was penicilin in 1928, so why and how was an antibiotic found in the bones of ancient Nubians?

Researchers found the answer in the beer making process itself. The type of bacteria that produces tetracycline can be found in the soil in hot and dry climates such as in Sudan. The clay jars that were used transferred the bacteria to the grains, indicating that the Nubians made the dough, baked it a little over a strong fire, and then made beer out of it. According to researchers, the Nubians drank the beer and gave the leftovers at the bottom of the jars to their children to eat. This explains why 90% of the bones analysed, including those of children younger than 24 months old, contained tetracycline.

It is also possible that drinking beer gave people energy. An ancient Egyptian medicine book even contains a list of recipes that clarify the medical benefits of beer. For example, beer paste could be used to seal wounds and beer incense to ease anal pain.

Scientists also believe that it was tetracycline that helped preserve the Nubian bones they studied since all the samples they examined were free from any contaminating materials.

THE PHARAOHS AND ALCOHOL

While Sumer had its beer deities, in ancient Egypt, it was wine that was considered to be a gift from the gods. Winemaking flourished under the Pharaohs and became part of everyday life, and consequently an integral part of the history of ancient Egypt and its kings. According to an ancient Egyptian saying: 'In water you see your own face, but in wine the heart of its garden' [1]

Wine in ancient Egypt was the drink of royals and nobles while beer was that of the common people. Wine always flowed at feasts and celebrations, and was given to commoners and soldiers only during holidays like the festivities held for Renenutet, the god of harvest, and Hathor, the goddess of love, beauty, and music.

On the west bank of the Nile, opposite the great city of Thebes was the Deir El Medina settlement where labourers working in the Valley of the Kings lived. It is believed that the labourers were given beer as a reward for their work, but it isn't clear whether everyone benefited from this compensation or if it was limited to supervisors. Several tablets have also been discovered indicating different kinds of alcohol.

According to Plutarch, a Greek historian who lived between 120 and 46 BC, the Pharaohs believed that the blood of those who fought against the gods was mixed with the soil of the earth to produce wine. This belief is linked to the ancient

---

1   Dr. Michael Poe Phd. http://www.touregypt.net/egypt-info/magazine-mag11012000-magf2.htm

Historical Background

Egyptian myth of the destruction of mankind. According to the myth, the god Ra sent his daughter Hathor to take vengeance on men who rebelled against him. But once Hathor started killing, she developed a taste for it and started killing men indiscriminately. The blood-thirsty goddess could no longer be stopped, so the gods devised a trick and gave her a red drink that looked like blood to calm her down. The drink is believed to have been wine, which the Pharaohs considered a holy drink reserved for the gods.

Most of the information we have about winemaking at the time comes from inscriptions found on jars, engraved drawings on the walls of the Pharaohs' tombs, written texts, or from laboratory analyses of jars used to store wine. The tomb engravings indicate 12 steps in the winemaking process. These drawings have been found in more than one burial site and do not necessarily date back to the same period in history. The 12 steps mark the most important stages; harvesting the grapes, crushing them, placing them in jars, storing them, and sometimes even over-consuming the resulting product. These depictions were probably not meant as a guide to making wine and were perhaps drawn by artists who had never seen wine being made. They probably copied the pictures from one tomb to the other, and some secondary stages in the process were never even illustrated.

As some of the colours can still be seen on the drawings in the Pharaohs' tombs, we can tell that they had different types of grapes; white, purple, green, red, even navy blue. The illustrations also show that wine was not just made from grapes but also from other fruits like figs, pomegranates, and dates. We still do not know how wine was made from other fruits, but the process most likely included the addition of sugar to help fermentation.

Planting vineyards was considered an agricultural achievement at the time because it required a great deal of resources and a large workforce. Vineyards often had religious names such as Homs Dja, meaning the drink of the god Horus, and were owned by nobles as a sign of luxury and proof of their privileged status.

The vines were always planted on a natural or manmade hill. Drawings found in tombs indicate that they were surrounded by stone and clay, and often by a wide water basin.

The vines rested on supports placed very closely together to minimise the fruits' exposure to the sun and therefore help maintain their moisture. The supports were themselves placed on thick ornate columns spaced far apart to allow labourers to move around with ease. Some workers dedicated their entire time to protecting the fruit from birds, and the 100 days before the harvest took on special importance because this could make the difference between good grapes and grapes of lesser quality.

Harvest season was probably at the end of the summer, when most vineyards would mature. The grapes were collected by hand rather than with a knife, and were placed in large baskets covered with vine leaves or palm leaves for protection. The men rested the baskets on their heads or shoulders to transport them to the press, and often transported two baskets at a time on their shoulders placing one on each side of a pole to keep them balanced.

The engraved drawings only show adult male labourers participating in harvest activities, no women or children. Once at the press, the grapes were placed in large round basins that could fit nine men standing. These basins were often made from granite, an impermeable and easy to clean material.

The men then crushed the grapes with their feet. This method was popular across the whole Mediterranean basin and considered to be superior to crushing the fruit using mill stones since the latter also crushes the pips and stems along with the fruit, adding a bitter taste to the wine.

Heavy vats made of hard stone (probably granite or schist) were built at the top of a hill with a rope hung above them to help the men keep their balance as they crushed the grapes. If no ropes were available, each worker would hold on to the waist of the person next to him with the last person on each end holding on to the wooden column. The whole process was accompanied by songs and music, with men singing and women playing instruments in glory of the harvest god Renenutet.

Once this stage was complete, the liquid was passed through a rectangular fabric sieve, knotted with a stick at each end. A labourer on each side twisted his stick the opposite direction to the person in front of him to sieve the juice. Another labourer stood behind each of the men to make sure the stick didn't snap backward.

The process therefore required four men. However, drawings show a fifth man in a vertical position. What was his function? Most likely, the artist was not familiar with the process or the fifth person was in charge of making sure the liquid coming out of the tissue ends up inside the jar where it would be kept for fermentation.

Many types of wine were produced this way, but there were three main methods. The first was wine made using the entire bunch of grapes, which were left to ferment whole. The resulting volume was small but it was sweet and could be stored for a long time. The second was made by manually crushing the grapes, and transforming a third of the juice to wine. The third was made by simply crushing the grapes.

There is no evidence that different types of grape juice were mixed to form a new wine as we do today to get sweet or dry white or red wine.

The fermentation stage is the process of transforming the sugar inside the grapes into alcohol by exposing the sugar enzymes to the natural yeast present in the skins, pips and stems of the grapes. The percentage of alcohol we find therefore changes according to the percentage of sugar in the grapes, with fermentation coming to a halt usually after reaching a level of 14% or 15% of alcohol. The remaining sugar adds sweetness to the wine.

Fermenting grapes for several days produces a light tasting wine while fermenting them for several weeks, and possibly heating the liquid, produces a strong-tasting wine with a high percentage of alcohol.

It is important to note that the colour of wine (red or white) does not depend on the colour of grape used in its production. Red wine is obtained by leaving the skins on the grapes, as well as the pips and stems, during fermentation. To produce white wine, the skins are removed.

When producing red wine, the Egyptians sieved the grape juice using pieces of cloth. They then immediately placed it in short conical jars with large openings. The narrow bottom of the jar allowed sediment to gather while the fermentation process went on, with the jars stored in caves.

Wine was usually stored for a few days until just before it turned to vinegar. A layer of straw, reeds or baked clay was placed on top of the mouth of the jar to allow the carbon dioxide to escape. This layer also provided insulation and prevented the wine from being polluted by the smell of the clay the jars were covered with before being transported to the caves.

The specifications of the wine, such as the year of production, the location of the vineyard, its owner, and often the type of wine, were engraved in the clay and inspected by specialised workers.

Scribes would prepare the jars before they were transported and would arrange them in long organized lines with old wines at the back and new ones at the front. The jars were either placed on stone or wooden platforms, or left to rest on the ground.

The lists discovered on the walls of tombs indicate that the ancient Egyptians had many different types of wine:

- *Irep Mehu:* A wine made in Lower Egypt or what is known as the Nile Delta. It was the most prominent winemaking region in ancient Egypt.
- *Irep Bes:* This wine was placed in a clay jar with a hollowed base known as an Abesh Jar. The jar was specifically made for the storing and ageing of wine.
- *Irep Imit:* A wine made in the village of Imit, north of Fakus in the Delta region.
- *Irep Dedjem:* A sweet tasting wine with a high percentage of alcohol due to the large amount of sugar fermented during its production. This wine was stored for long periods of time and was sweetened by adding dried fruits and honey, which reactivated the fermentation process. At times, ripe dried grapes would also be added to the liquid to increase sugar levels and extend the life of the wine.

Other wines were produced by mixing two or more types of fruits but very little information is available about them. All we know is that they existed and were mixed shortly before being consumed.

CHAPTER II

Religious Background

Who is the God of Alcohol?

Alcohol in Judaism

Alcohol in Buddhism

Alcohol in Christianity

Alcohol in Islam

WHO IS THE GOD OF ALCOHOL?

We often associate the three great monotheistic religions with the Middle East. Judaism, Christianity and Islam have each developed their own traditions and customs related to alcohol. But apart from being the cradle of monotheism, the region, and more precisely the Levant (modern day Syria, Lebanon and Palestine) was an integral part of the ancient Graeco-Roman world, and enjoyed linguistic, cultural and religious affinities with the rest of the Mediterranean basin.

The ancient Greek god of wine is Dionysus. He is the hero of many myths and has inspired rituals that celebrate joy and ecstasy in his name. He was also known as Bacchus to the Romans.

In Greek mythology, the twelve Olympians were the major deities who lived on Mount Olympus where the Pantheon was located. Dionysus was the last of these twelve. Dionysus' father was the almighty Zeus, ruler of the Olympians, his mother was a mortal, the daughter of Cadmus, the king of Thebes, a Greek city.

According to the myth, while she was pregnant, Cadmus' daughter Semele asked Zeus to prove his divinity to her by showing her his glory as the almighty god of thunder and lightning. However, mere mortals cannot see a deity in the fullness of his glory without dying and Semele's incinerated body fell to the earth. But, Zeus saved the infant Dionysus from his mother's womb and sewed him into his own thigh. Dionysus was born a few months later and is therefore known as the "twice-born": born the first

(Left) Bacchus, the ancient Roman god of wine.

time out of his mother's womb and the second out of his father's thigh.

This story may also explain the origins of the expression – still current in French - "to think yourself born from Jupiter's thigh"[(2)]. The idiom is used to describe people who think highly of themselves.

Dionysus' adolescence was troubled and very eventful. He was kidnapped by pirates and was only released after performing a series of miracles. He also wanted to rescue his mother from the underworld. With a guide, he descended

---

2   «se croire sorti de la cuisse de Jupiter»

to the bottomless pool of Lerne, north of the city of Argos in Greece, rescued his mother, and carried her to Mount Olympus. Semele was afterwards known as Thyone and Dionysus's actions are considered a symbol of transition from adolescence to adulthood.

Dionysus is often called the Wanderer who never settles down and appears out of nowhere. He appears in his mortal state to spread his cult, and can transcend death through wine. Another name for Dionysus is the Liberator who frees men from themselves through ecstasy and wine, and his ability to connect the living and the dead. His objective as a deity is to free men from their cares and fears through the music he plays on his flute. While many wine-filled festivities were held to honour him, the most important are the Bacchanals. Held in ancient Greece, the Bacchanals were religious festivals held to honour Bacchus, the god of wine, inebriation, and above all, sexual freedom. The festivals themselves were probably inspired by more ancient religious rituals. However, the term Bacchanals mostly refers to the gatherings held in Italy around 300 BC on March 16 and 17. At first, they were secret and limited to women. They later became public and were celebrated in Egypt and across the Greek-speaking world, and were especially popular in Rome. They lasted three to five days depending on the region, and involved theatrical shows accompanied by religious rituals. Nonetheless, the festivals gained a bad reputation as gatherings based on chaos, sex, drunkenness, and debauchery. They were viewed with special suspicion in Rome where they were held in secret.

Men, pretending to be pious, secretly ran alongside the women holding their torches to the Tiber, Rome's sacred river, to participate in the hedonistic parties. The women placed certain conditions for men to join, including for them to be under 20 years old, and therefore easier to train and integrate. Even elite citizens participated in the Bacchanals, which grew so large that these secret gatherings were considered a threat by the authorities. However, the secret was exposed when Hispala, a Roman courtesan, told her lover Publius about their reality to protect him from his mother who was encouraging him to join the gatherings. Publius listened to his mistress, thus angering his mother and her husband who retaliated by kicking him out. He sought refuge with his aunt who urged him to share his story with the ruler. An investigation was launched and a report was submitted to the senate. The latter issued orders to reward whomever had information about the gatherings.

In 186 BC, the Bacchanals were banned by the authorities and 7,000 participants were sentenced to death. The Bacchanals were prohibited for about a century until Rome's Julius Caesar (100-49 BC) revived them. Echoes of them live on in the form of modern day carnivals.

Perhaps the most famous temple dedicated to Bacchus is in the town of Baalbek in modern day Lebanon. The temple, also known as the "small temple", sits next to the Temple of Jupiter and was built between 200 and 150 BC. At the temple's entrance are carvings of grape vines, opium poppies, and Bacchic scenes indicating the identity of the god the temple was dedicated to.

ALCOHOL IN JUDAISM

The Jewish sacred texts describe wine as a drink that brings joy to both God and humans. In fact, all the sacrifices made at Solomon's Temple were accompanied by wine, and rabbis prayed the *Hagafen* to bless wine, considered to be the best of all alcoholic drinks.

Judaism believes in the importance of the human body, and teaches the need to preserve it and protect it from any disfigurement or corruption because the body ultimately returns to God. Followers of the Jewish faith must therefore avoid dangerous activities that might undermine their health, including the abuse of alcohol. Alcohol is not prohibited in Judaism as long as it doesn't interfere with religious rites and doesn't harm the body. Nonetheless, many rabbis warn against drinking as a precautionary measure to avoid social, legal, and medical problems in their communities.

That said, drinking alcohol, sometimes even in large quantities, is common in some conservative Jewish communities. Men are required to "get drunk" on Purim until they can no longer recognise the difference between the Hebrew words Haman (cursed) and Mordechai (blessed). Once they are at this stage, they are said to have attained *Atziluth*, the world of truth and the highest level in the Tree of Life where opposites unite.

The holiday of Purim is inspired from a story in the Bible when Esther miraculously saved the Jewish people from the Persian minister Haman's plan to get rid of them. The holiday

Religious Background

is celebrated every year in February or March according to the Gregorian calendar.

The story goes that Mordechai belonged to one of the two tribes that founded the ancient Jewish kingdom before it was destroyed by Nebuchadnezzar . As part of the Jewish elite, he was taken into exile in the Persian kingdom. However, Mordechai gained an esteemed position in the Persian court. This was how he discovered Haman's plot against the Jews.

Another Jewish occasion often accompanied by alcohol is the *Sim'hat Torah*, during which the last annual reading of the Torah is celebrated.

During the *Farbrengen* gatherings, Hasidic Jews drink to the point of hallucination. They gather and drink to lift their spirits, bring people closer together, contemplate, and self-examine.

In some Hasidic movements, such as the Chabad, alcohol is used as a tool that helps connect with God and foster the spirit of brotherhood within the Jewish community. Private gatherings called *tisch* are organised where people drink vodka, and read or sing the Torah.

Wine, in particular, plays an important role in most Jewish religious rites. Most important is the *Kiddush*, a prayer recited to bless wine or grape juice at the start of celebrations, and used to ask God for the ability to keep the 613 *mitzvot* (commandments).

If wine is not available, any other alcoholic drink like beer, or even bread can be used instead. During the *Kiddush*, the most senior person in the room raises a glass of wine (half the size of a glass of water) and recites the prayer out loud. He then drinks half the glass and offers the other half to those present to taste. The cup used is usually ornate and made of silver. It is placed on a table covered by an elegant cloth, and next to it are placed a basket containing two pieces of bread wrapped in cloth and two candles.

The *Kiddush* rites can be observed on various holidays, but are mainly held on *Shabbat*, the Jewish Sabbath. Shabbat starts on Friday after sundown and ends on Saturday after stars appear in the sky. After that, the *Kiddush* prayer is recited three times at specific hours. A different request is made with each prayer and the last prayer to conclude the *Shabbat* is called *Havdallah*.

An essential Jewish holiday that must be mentioned is Passover. It celebrates the passage of the Jewish people from slavery under the Pharaohs to freedom under the leadership of Moses. As well as having a religious importance, Passover celebrates freedom and the establishment of the Jewish people. On the eve of the holiday, the stages of Exodus are told and every person sat at the table drinks four shots of wine (or grape juice) at certain times throughout the meal.

In Hasidic Judaism, a movement that began in the 18th century in Eastern Europe, rabbis emphasise the importance of uniting with God through happiness and joy, and singing and dancing. Rabbis in this movement inherit their role and are famous for drinking a great deal of vodka during special occasions to induce hallucinations. This is a contrast with the hard life Hasidic rabbis used to live: one of austerity, prayer, contemplation, and bathing in freezing Russian waters.

Kabbalists are practitioners of the discipline of Kabbala, a collection of complex and esoteric Jewish beliefs. The difficult study of Kabbala was limited to married students of the Talmud such as Isaac of Acco and Abraham Abulafia. These scholars encouraged meditation by drinking a full glass of a special type of wine (known as Avicenna wine), known for its ability to bring ecstasy and help contemplate complicated philosophical issues. As for the way this wine is made, the recipe has long remained a secret.

ALCOHOL IN BUDDHISM

Buddhism, at least at its foundation, started as a movement of reform that sought to challenge regressive notions in Indian philosophy. For centuries, Indians believed in two main concepts: the first was the reincarnation of the individual soul in the immortal soul, and the second was the continuous rebirth of the soul. Buddhism, in fact, is in many ways more a philosophy than a religion. It is a system for the salvation of the soul. The Buddha focused his teachings on finding the road to salvation, and Buddhism first appeared in the form of a community of monks who followed the Buddha's teachings. They were homeless and penniless, and did not take on the role of priests. It was their example that led others to adopt the Buddha's philosophy for salvation.

The Buddha was reportedly born to Queen Maya and King

(Above) Giant Buddha carved in stone in the Tibet mountains

Suddhodana around 560 BC, and died approximately 80 years later. He has many names but the most important one is the Awakened.

As a young man, the Buddha lived a calm and happy life. However, after discovering that his happiness was an illusion born out of his sheltered life, he decided to travel and went to extremes to find peace. He lived a life of extreme poverty and pushed his body to its limits. For example, he refused to sit and stayed crouched for long periods of time. He slept on a bed of thorns and ate only one grain of rice a day. However, none of his attempts led him to his soul's salvation. Emaciated and frail, he realised that self-torture was useless, and that living a life of austerity hadn't helped him any more than living in luxury. It was then that he realised the importance of the Middle Way.

He said: "Monks, these two extremes should not be followed by one who has gone forth into homelessness. What two? The pursuit of sensual happiness in sensual pleasures, which is low, vulgar, the way of worldlings, ignoble, unbeneficial; and the pursuit of self-mortification, which is painful, ignoble, unbeneficial. Without veering toward either of these extremes, the Tathagata has awakened to the middle way, which gives rise to vision, which gives rise to knowledge, and leads to peace, to direct knowledge, to enlightenment, to Nibbana."[3]

As for alcohol, Buddhists are encouraged not to drink it because it does not go with the Buddha's teachings. Alcohol

---

3   "Buddhism" by Henri Arvon (Arabic edition).

corrupts the human spirit, which is of immense value to humans. Buddhists must work hard and meditate to control their spirits.

Buddhism offers five commandments in the form of guiding principles. One of them clearly indicates that Buddhists must not drink alcohol because an awakened mind is essential to the Buddhist philosophy. A person must always be aware of changes in their mind and body, but alcohol corrupts thoughts and prevents men from truly practicing their beliefs.

Of course, this is if a person is strictly abiding by the Buddha's teachings. We see many Buddhists who do drink or see no clear religious reason not to drink. Even in countries with a Buddhist majority and where Buddhism is taught at school, you can find people drinking alcohol. Buddhism has also recently become popular in the West where very few people follow its principles on alcohol to the letter. This tolerance and absence of guilt with regards to alcohol can be traced back to two main points that are at the core of Buddhism. They provide an intellectual cover for wine lovers:

The first is the principle of the Middle Way. Alcohol is one of life's pleasures and should not be consumed to the point of addiction in search of happiness. True happiness comes from confronting problems and challenges, and from solving them through patience and meditation. Therefore, there is no need to give up alcohol completely. Humans need the joy that it gives them in their daily lives. To consume alcohol with moderation reflects the Middle Way the Buddha taught.

(Above) Noah and his family stepping out of the ark after the flood.

(Below) Noah inebriated as imagined by Michael Angelo on the ceiling of the Sistine Chapel, the Vatican.

The Milk of Lions - A History of Alcohol in the Middle East

(Above) An Assyrian form relief Nineveh depicts Ashurbanipal and his queen drinking wine.

(Left) Hammurabi lifts his hand to the god of justice who hands him the code that later becomes known by his name. The code is carved into the bottom of a stele discovered in Iran in 1951.

(Above) Gilgamesh on the right mourning his friend Enkidu.

(Right) Map showing the ancient geography of the region, with the Nubian areas appearing in the north.

The Milk of Lions - A History of Alcohol in the Middle East

(Left) Woman fermenting beer, Museum of Cairo.

(Below) An ancient Nubian woman serving beer to her husband.

(Opposite top) Removing the impurities from the grape juice.

(Opposite bottom) The façade of Hathor's temple in Abu Simbel.

(Above) Drawings of the harvesting and crushing of grapes on the walls of a temple in Thebes, ancient Egypt.

(Below) Transporting grapes to the press.

(Above) Harvest and arranging jars to be transported on the Nile.

(Below) Arrangement of jars and noting down wine specifications.

The Milk of Lions - A History of Alcohol in the Middle East

(Above) Entrance to the temple of Bacchus in Baalbek, Lebanon.
(Left) Dyonysus, the Greek god of wine.
(Below) Representation of the Bacchanals, Louvre Museum.

This again falls in line with the passage in the Psalms:

"...and wine to gladden the heart of man."

Psalms (5: 104)

The second point is that of Karma. The principle of Karma states that every person has their own karma that makes them responsible for their actions. Drinking can be synonymous with lack of responsibility, and can therefore result in negative karma.

Karma is in fact a popular concept in many Indian religions from Hinduism to Sikhism, and Buddhism. It means that a person's good deeds or bad deeds while alive will have moral consequences. No matter the source of an action, word, or idea, whether good or bad, if done with awareness and prior understanding, it will have certain consequences. These consequences are like fruit that grow and mature until they fall. Then, their owner is either rewarded or punished. Karma is therefore the principle of reward and punishment. Alcohol falls within this system for many Buddhists. If they abuse it, they will be punished. If they show moderation, they are rewarded.

ALCOHOL IN CHRISTIANITY

Christianity's relationship with wine is clear. Wine is at the heart of the Christian faith and symbolises Christ's blood given to his people during mass as the priest prays:

This cup is the new covenant in my blood, which is poured out for you.

In fact, Christ first revealed his divinity through wine when he performed his first miracle at the marriage at Cana:

And the third day there was a marriage in Cana of Galilee; and the mother of Jesus was there: And both Jesus was called, and his disciples, to the marriage. And when they wanted wine, the mother of Jesus saith unto him, They have no wine. Jesus saith unto her, Woman, what have I to do with thee? mine hour is not yet come. His mother saith unto the servants, Whatsoever he saith unto you, do it.

And there were set there six waterpots of stone, after the manner of the purifying of the Jews, containing two or three firkins apiece. Jesus saith unto them, Fill the waterpots with water. And they filled them up to the brim. And he saith unto them, Draw out now, and bear unto the governor of the feast. And they bare it. When the ruler of the feast had tasted the water that was made wine, and knew not whence it was: (but the servants which drew the water knew; the governor of the feast called the bridegroom, And saith unto him, Every man at the beginning doth set

> *forth good wine; and when men have well drunk, then that which is worse: but thou hast kept the good wine until now. This beginning of miracles did Jesus in Cana of Galilee, and manifested forth his glory; and his disciples believed on him*
>
> (John 2:1-11)

Throughout his teachings, Jesus also used wine as an example for good behaviour:

> *No man putteth a piece of new cloth unto an old garment, for that which is put in to fill it up taketh from the garment, and the rent is made worse. Neither do men put new wine into old bottles: else the bottles break, and the wine runneth out, and the bottles perish: but they put new wine into new bottles, and both are preserved.*
> (Matthew 9:16-17)

On the eve of his crucifixion, he gathered his disciples for the last supper, and…

> *And as they were eating, Jesus took bread, and blessed it, and brake it, and gave it to the disciples, and said, Take, eat; this is my body.*
>
> *And he took the cup, and gave thanks, and gave it to them, saying, Drink ye all of it; For this is my blood of the new testament, which is shed for many for the remission of*

> sins. But I say unto you, I will not drink henceforth of this fruit of the vine, until that day when I drink it new with you in my Father's kingdom.

In fact, the Eucharist[4], or communion, is one of the most important sacraments in Christianity. It reminds Christians of Jesus' last supper with his disciples before he was crucified. The celebration is marked by eating a small piece of bread (also known as altar bread) that represents the body of Christ. The bread can be dipped into some wine, which represents the blood of Christ. During this sacred moment, Christians believe that the bread and the wine turn into the body and blood of Christ. By consuming them, they implicitly eat this body and drink this blood. It is an essential rite and the key objective of the mass.

The wine priests drink during the Eucharist is usually sweet with a high percentage of sugar. This wine is produced at monasteries rather than being sourced commercially. It is preferred to other types of wine because it is easier to store and keep.

In the First Epistle of Paul to Timothy, Paul says:

> *Drink no longer water, but use a little wine for thy stomach's sake and thine often infirmities.*
>
> (1 Timothy 5:23)

---

4 The term Eucharist is of Greek origin and means "to give thanks".

Religious Background

This was advice given by Jesus' foremost disciple.

According to the Bible, Jesus was born in Palestine and was crucified under the authority of the Roman Empire. For the Romans, drinking wine was part of everyday life. Wine was available to everyone; men, women, and even children. It was considered an essential part of the diet and even had medical uses. Wine was available at all occasions and holidays, and was stored in towers and behind walls the same as other types of food and drink. Wine was also an essential commercial good that could be traded for wheat, barley, and cereal. In fact, men in the Roman Empire probably used to drink about one litre of wine a day on average.

The Romans, and the Greeks before them, would sometimes dilute the wine with water at various ratios.

Western societies have been significantly influenced by Christian culture. Regardless of political systems, Western countries tend to place restrictions on alcohol for social and public health reasons rather than for religious reasons. Alcohol not only has medical uses in these communities, helping get through the harsh weather conditions of northern Europe, but is also considered an essential part of the diet and of social relations.

When it comes to table etiquette, wine is the most important factor. Every course is paired with a different wine, either to help increase people's appetites, to help savour the food, or to help digest it. Different types of meat and fish are paired with different types of wine, and the same is true for desserts and fruit. Some wines should be drunk in the morning and others in the afternoon. The repertoire of the types of wine and the different ways to drink them is endless.

In terms of social relations, wine and alcohol are always present. Whether the occasion is happy or sad, alcohol is used to deepen and strengthen social ties.

At feasts or at small meals, in palaces and cottages, wine and alcohol are often placed on the table even before water is provided.

This wine-centred culture is at its essence a Christian culture.

ALCOHOL IN ISLAM

Wine was the drink of choice in the Arabian Peninsula well before Islam. During this time, known as the Age of ignorance , merchants from Damascus sold quality wine to the merchants of Mecca, who would drink it as they sat down for rich and abundant meals. In addition to this, the Peninsula also had its own vineyards and wine presses; in Yemen, Tihamah, Taif, Yathrib, and Qadi al-Qira. According to the fourth century book *Qutb al-Surur fi Awsaf al Anbitha wal-Khumur* (an encyclopaedic work on wine dating to the 4th century AH/9th century AD), the cultivation of the vine, and with it, the production of wine, was spreading in the Arabian Peninsula even before the advent of Islam.

At the very beginning of Islam, the prophet Muhammad did not declare a strict position regarding alcohol. In fact, he and his followers drank alcohol just as the pagans did during Islam's first 13 years in Mecca. They continued to drink even three to eight years (accounts differ on this point) after their migration to Yathrib, which is better known today as Medina. (Qamus al-Turath). It should be noted that the Qur'an was revealed over a period of several years, and verses were often 'revealed' from God in response to specific circumstances facing the fledgling Muslim community, as the history of Qur'anic verses relating to alcohol demonstrates.

Muslims who were used to drinking before converting to Islam continued to drink and trade in wine, and would take it with them to battle. The Holy Qur'an itself first praised the sources of wine:

And from the fruit of palm trees and vines you derive intoxicants as well as goodly provision.
In this is a sign for a people who understand
(The Bees: 67)

It also describes rivers in paradise:

The likeness of the Garden promised to the pious is this: in it are rivers of water, not brackish, and rivers of milk, unchanging in taste, and rivers of wine, delicious to them who drink it, and rivers of honey, pure and limpid.
(Muhammad: 15)

The Qur'an even tempted believers with a special drink in paradise:

But the righteous shall drink from a cup [of wine] mixed with choicest fragrance
(Man: 5)

There shall pass among them a cup [of wine] from a fountain,
Crystal clear, a delight to those who drink it;
(Arrayed in Ranks: 45, 46)

Indeed, it goes so far as to promise a wine that is never-ending, and headache free:

Causing them neither ache nor intoxication
(Calamity: 19)

After his followers in Medina asked him about wine, the Prophet answered:

Say: "In them both lies grave sin, though some benefit, to mankind. But their sin is more grave than their benefit
(The Cow: 219)

After this verse was revealed from God, some believers chose to give up alcohol while others continued to drink. Then it happened that some of the Prophet's first followers were drinking at the house of Abd al-Rahman ibn 'Awf and it was time for them to pray. One of them started to read the verse: *Say, "O disbelievers, I do not worship what you worship*, but mistakenly omitted the *"not"*. A verse was then revealed to the Prophet prohibiting prayer while drunk:

O believers, do not come near to prayer when you are drunk, until you know what you are saying
(Women: 43)

Some believers considered this verse to be a confirmation of the one revealed before it and stopped drinking. Others, on the other hand, continued to drink but not during prayer times. When people were called to prayer, they were in fact warned, *"Approach not prayer when you are in a drunken state."*

Many events resulting from drunkenness occurred after this verse was revealed, causing an array of political problems. The Prophet felt concerned and Muslim leaders wanted a solution. Two verses were then revealed that called for the avoidance of alcohol:

> *O believers, wine and gambling, idols and diving arrows are an abhorrence, the work of Satan. So keep away from it, that you may prevail. Satan only desires to arouse discord and hatred among you with wine and gambling, and to deter you from the mention of God and from prayer. Will you desist?*
>
> (The Table: 90, 91)

Some scholars see these two verses as evidence that Islam prohibits drinking alcohol. However, some find room for interpretation. According to Syrian scholar Hadi al-Alawi:

> *"The text of the two verses is not complete. 'So keep away from it, that you may prevail' can be understood as a preference to avoid alcohol while taking into consideration individual circumstances. Exclusions in the Qur'an are usually assertive and come in two forms: either a clear prohibition is stated like in the case of prohibiting eating blood, pork, and dead animals, and forbidding incest, or*

the act is paired with punishment as in the cases of adultery, theft, and murder. As for alcohol, there is no statement of prohibition and no punishment is mentioned. The verses call for avoiding alcohol, which indicates hesitation in completely forbidding the act." [5]

Those who completely disagree with this view refuse any indication of hesitation. They support interpretations that see the call to "keep away" as more assertive than prohibition.

According to fatwa resources on the website Islamweb, any hesitation regarding alcohol in Islam ended when the below verse was revealed:

O believers, wine and gambling, idols and diving arrows are an abhorrence, the work of Satan. So keep away from it, that you may prevail.

(The Table: 90)

For some, this is a clear indication that alcohol is forbidden. Others even go as far as saying, "there is nothing Allah has prohibited more than wine."

Some read the below as evidence of absolute prohibition:
- The use of "only";
- Comparing drinking alcohol to idolatry;
- Describing drinking as "abhorrence";
- Describing drinking as the "work of Satan";

---

5   Hadi Alomari (1933-1998): Arabic thinker born in Baghdad.

- Ordering to "keep away from it";
- The avoidance of alcohol is considered a success, and drinking a failure;
- Linking alcohol to other evils such as gambling and hatred, which keep believers from the remembrance of Allah and from prayer, *"Will you desist?"* (The Table: 91). Avoiding alcohol is consequently made similar to abstaining from other forbidden actions. If believers are willing to drink, they may be willing to ignore other commandments as well

In the *Sunnah*, the record of the Prophet's teachings, many *Hadiths* (sayings attributed to the Prophet) tackle the issue of alcohol:

> *Ibn 'Umar reported the Prophet as saying: "Every intoxicant is Khamr [alcohol] and every intoxicant is forbidden."*
> (Sahih Muslim)

Abu Hurayrah reported the Prophet as saying: *"no one who drinks wine is a believer at the moment when he is drinking it,"* meaning no person is a true believer when they are drinking wine.

Ahmad reported on the authority of Ibn 'Abbas that the Prophet said: *"Gabriel came to me and said, 'O Muhammad, Allah has cursed wine, and whoever presses it for another, presses it for himself, drinks it, carries it, accepts its delivery, sells it, buys it, pours it for another or pours it for himself.'"*

Some believe that alcohol harms a person's faith, body, mind, finances, community, and family.

However, questions have long been asked about the use of the term *khamr* in the Qur'an and the Hadiths. Does it mean wine from grapes only or does it also include other types of wine, and by extension, other types of alcohol? In the city of Kufa, religious aristocrats and the Prophet's companions allowed a specific drink called *nabith* (what we know as wine). However, the three great scholars of Islamic law Malik, al-Shafi'I, and Ibn Hanbal considered all intoxicants to be alcohol and alcohol to be prohibited in the Qur'an, including all wines. Imam Abu Hanifah, on the other hand, interpreted the term *khamr* in the Qur'anic verses to be grape juice.

Arabic texts define *khamr* as intoxicating grape juice that distracts the mind. It only refers to drinks made from grapes and Arabic, considers the words "grape" and *khamr* to be synonyms. Surat Yusuf in the Qur'an uses the Arabic word *khamr*:

> "Indeed, I have seen myself [in a dream] pressing grapes."
> (Yusuf: 36)

Nabith is a different term that reflects the transfer of an item (the verb *nabatha* in Arabic means 'to dispose of'). The traditional winemaking process includes the transfer of dates, raisins or grapes in a water filled container, after which the mixture is left to ferment until it becomes alcoholic.

It should be noted that 100 years after the *Hijra* (Muhammad and his followers' flight from Mecca to Medina) in 718 AD, wine was still available and drinking it was acceptable in the northern parts of Africa. To control its consumption, the Caliph Umar bin Abdul Aziz tasked Ismail ibn Abi al-Muhajir with establishing jurisprudence over the consumption of wine and the latter appointed scholars (Abdulrahman bin Rafi'm, Saad bin Saud al-Tujibi, etc.) who explained to believers the difference between what was prohibited and what was allowed (Ibn Athari). The prohibition of alcohol had not in fact spread to all parts of the Muslim world even 100 years after the Hijra.

CHAPTER III

Alcohol in the Arab World

Alcohol in the Arab World
The Age of Ignorance Period
The Dawn of Islam
The Abbasid Period
The Andalusian Period
The Mamluk and Ottoman Period
Renaissance

ALCOHOL IN THE ARAB WORLD

The archaeological remains of many ancient civilizations include pottery and jars where beer or wine would have been kept. The Sumerians, Egyptians, Greeks, Romans, and many others have left physical objects attesting the consumption of alcoholic drinks. Ancient Arabic-speaking civilizations have not. However, the main traces these civilizations have left from the period both before and after Islam take the form of poetry. Poetry has always had a preponderant place in Arabic literature, more so than other forms of literature, and even today remains the most prestigious genre. And when it comes to wine, Arabic poetry is some of the best ever written on the subject. The eloquence and mastery of Arabic poetry would not be the same without having the theme of wine and alcohol at its core. Without them, the music and the ecstasy in the verses would be nothing but mere empty flattery and flirtation.

The truth is not being fully told in the Arab world. Historians sometimes overlook some aspects of history, either to please rulers, or for religious reasons, or both. Nonetheless, traces live on in the form of whispers and poetry telling of taboo themes like same-sex love, or even dark themes like massacres. Historians have not always passed down the full picture, but Arabic poetry has faithfully attested to the deep and ancient relationship of Arab culture with alcohol. Various sources seem to agree on the same unequivocal fact. It can even be said that this ancient poetry has been essential, even if unintentionally so, in keeping a record of the daily life of the community.

(Right) A relief showing the Tree of Life, 7th century BC, Babylon, Iraq.

History can be discerned through the poets' verses and their intended audience. The detailed descriptions of joy, sadness, battle, flirtation, etc. have helped paint, and preserve, an image of the past from which we can draw lessons. Poetry is a mirror for society, with all its joys, mores, spontaneity, sadness, humiliations, decadence, moral codes etc. A poet writing about alcohol does not have the same inhibitions as one writing about society or politics. His feelings about alcohol are pure, clear, and untroubled. They are true. The best way to learn about the culture of drinking in the Arab world is to read the poems, and review the lives of the poets from the start of the Age of Ignorance period until today.

THE AGE OF IGNORANCE
Arabia in the period circa 400 BC - AD 610, referred to by Islamic historians as the "Jahiliyya", running up to before the advent of Islam in 610 AD

In the era before the coming of Islam, known as the Age of Ignorance (or sometimes, the Jahiliyya Period), the custom of drinking alcohol was very common, and was an indication of luxury, pride and generosity. Alcohol was often the subject of poetry, and it was not unusual for its description to be linked to that of a loved one, to regret, or to nostalgia over the traces left by long-departed loved ones. Many poets were addicted to alcohol and Arabs continued to drink to excess, with merchants trading in it without restriction well after the birth of Islam. Muslims who had been accustomed to drinking alcohol before converting to Islam continued to do so afterwards, or at least until the Prophet received divine inspiration to prohibit drinking following the battles of Badr[6] and Uhud[7]. The story narrated in the Hadiths (a collection of traditions containing sayings of the prophet Muhammad) state that a number of believers took alcohol with them to the Battle of Uhud and were subsequently killed. It was after this incident that the Qur'anic verses banning the consumption of spirits were revealed to the Prophet Muhammad. Combatants in fact believed that

---

6   A battle won by Muslims in 624 AD, named after a well on the road to Mecca.
7   A battle the Muslims lost on 625 AD that took place in a mountainous area near Medina

consuming alcohol ahead of battle would increase their zeal and bloodlust, helping them to triumph[8] . In the words of the poet Hassan Ibn Thabit:

To drink it would make you king ... A roaring lion when armies meet

Many Arabs had an intricate relationship with alcohol during this period, and some even hoped to be reunited with it after death, as shown below in the words of Abu Mihjan al-Thaqafi - himself a dedicated drinker:

When I die, bury me at the roots of the vine... Let its water soak my bones
I fear to miss its sweetness when I am gone. The vast arid desert is no place for me...

Poets spoke of ecstasy and splendour, of being transported out of this world into a new one where they are kings and where they are brave:

When I drink ... I rule the castles of Khawarnaq and Sudair[9]
When I am sober ... I can only herd sheep and camels

---

8   Emile Nassif, Collection of Literature on Spirits and Gatherings around them, (al-Jil)
9   Two castles of King Naaman of Iraq

The kiss of a lover is compared to aged wine and its radiance is described as it mixes with rain water in silver jugs:

The taste of her lips, has the sweetness of wine ... flowing
    cup that loosen your dress
They are raindrops falling into silver jugs ... for which
    merchants would pay a precious price[10]

The scholar Ibn Qutaybah mentions that three tribal chiefs in the Age of Ignorance period committed suicide by drinking pure, unmixed alcohol: Zuhayr Ibn Janab, Abu Baraa al-Amiri, and Umar bin Kulthum. They had become so overwhelmed with anger over the hurt they had endured. Too proud, they chose to die in dignity rather than endure humiliation. In fact, it was not unknown for noblemen who fell hostage to their enemies and had no hope of survival to ask their captors to give them a dignified death by allowing them to drink wine before being killed[11]. The following pages provide a glimpse into Jahiliyya poetry on wine.

Al-Muhalhel: Wine today... serious matters tomorrow

Uday bin Rabi'a, also known as Abu Layla and Al-Muhalhel, was the uncle of the poet Imru' al-Qais and the grandfather of the tribe leader Amr Ibn Kulthum. He was daring, and

---

10 Farukh, Umar. Al-Manhaj al-Jadid fi al-Adab al-'Arabi
11 Al-Bustani, Butrus. Udaba al-'arab

like other princes, dedicated his days to drinking, pleasure, and women. His brother Kulaib, called him a "ladies' man". Uday took no interest in wars or conquests because his brother fulfilled those duties. One day, Uday was drinking and gambling with his cousin Hammam when the latter's chambermaid told him that al-Jassass had killed his brother Kulaib and that his father had sent a horse for him to follow into battle. Uday responded:

"The hand of Jassass is shorter than you think." He then continued drinking until he drank himself into a stupor and said: "I drink today, I tend to serious matters tomorrow". He added:

Leave me, this drinker will not be sober today ... nor tomorrow, and how closer today is than tomorrow
My vision has been blurred by wine ... It is all I care about and all I have patience for .

He continued this way until he was completely inebriated, and then rode to Yemen.

Imru' al-Qais

Imru' al-Qais was born in Najd, his mother was al-Muhalhel's sister. His name means "man of force" and, as the son of a king, he was raised in luxury and leisure. He was a good-looking man with a gift for poetry; in all its metres. He also tackled daring subjects in his work, including his father's nose. His father, who was not happy with his son's chosen vocation, ordered him to stop writing. When Imru' al-Qais refused, his father banished him. After that, he travelled with his friends and camped wherever they could find water. There, they would hunt, eat, drink wine, recite poetry and sing. They would stay until the water dried up and Imru' al-Qais would then lead them to another source. One day, while drinking and playing dice with a friend, he received news of his father's death. He said:

He let me stray when I was small, and now that I am grown he has burdened me with his blood. There will be no alertness today, and no drunkenness tomorrow.

He then quoted his uncle al-Muhalhel and said: "I drink today, I tend to serious matters tomorrow." This quote has now become famous throughout the Arabic-speaking world.

During the Age of Ignorance, when a member of the tribe was killed, it was customary to refrain from drinking and avoid the company of women until the murder was avenged.

To my wine I can return, for occupied I was with a most important matter [of avenging a death]

Amr Ibn Kulthum

Amr Ibn Kulthum was a member of the Taghlib tribe from al-Forat Island. His father was a respected and admired tribe leader, and Amr grew up proud of his parents and his people. According to the Kitab al-Aghani ("The Book of Songs"), which is an encyclopaedic collection of poems and songs compiled in the 10th century, Amr Ibn Kulthum became their leader at 24 years old.

He wrote seven poems that were considered the finest of pre-Islamic poetry. Arabs called them the seven linked poems because they were linked together like pearls on a necklace. The leaders of the Quraysh tribe, whenever they heard these poems at the open market known as Souk Okaz, referred to them as the poems that "lingered" in the mind.

Amr Ibn Kulthum described wine and its affect in one of his famous poems:

> *Up with the bowl! Give us our dawn draught*
> *And do not spare the wines of al-Andarina[12],*
> *The brightly sparkling, as if by saffron were in them*
> *Whenever the mulled water is mingled with them,*
> *That swing the hotly desirous from his passion*
> *When he has tasted them to gentle mellowness;*
> *You see the skinflint miser, when the cup's passed him,*
> *Suddenly holds his prized property in derision[13].*

---

12 A village located in the south of the city of Aleppo in Syria.
13 https://www.poemhunter.com/best-poems/amr-ibn-kulthum/ode-13/

Antarah Ibn Shaddad

Antarah Ibn Shaddad was born a slave and grew up herding his father's camels. However, he became a legend thanks to his horsemanship and courage, great feats, and compassion for widows and orphans. He sided with the oppressed and avenged them, and was the ideal image of a "perfect knight". All of these admirable traits, however, stemmed from one event in his life: his love for Abla. He fell in love with his cousin Ablah, but could not marry her because of his social position. The love story between "Antar and Abla" has been the source of inspiration for both Arabic and non-arabic works of art.

Four of his verses can summarize his view on drinking:

> *And, verily, I have drunk wine after the midday heats have subsided, buying it with the bright stamped coin.*
> *From a glass, yellow with the lines of the glass-cutter on it, which was accompanied by a white-stoppered bottle on the left-hand side.*
> *And when I have drunk, verily, I am the squanderer of my property, and my honour is great, and is not sullied.*
> *And when I have become sober, I do not diminish in my generosity, and as you know, so are my qualities and my liberality.*[14]

In these verses, he describes how drinking makes him overly

---
14 http://www.sacred-texts.com/isl/hanged/hanged2.htm

generous but does not impact his honour. His values remain the same when he is drunk as when sober, and his listeners should not assume his generosity is the result of drinking[15].

Al-A'sha… or the Damp Grave

The story goes that the ruler of al-Yamama, a region in Najd in the Arab Peninsula, passed by the grave of al-A'sha and found it to be damp. When he asked why, he learned that young men from the village of Manfuha (al-A'sha's native village) were gathering around the grave, drinking, and pouring their drinks on the grave to remember the poet's love of alcohol when he was alive.

He was known for singing his poetry and for the rhyme and rhythm in his verses. His poems travelled far and were passed on by storytellers and sung by singers. Very few of his poems fail to mention alcohol and its effects, drinking sessions, or regret. He developed a personality around alcohol that distinguished him for other pre-Islamic poets. But he didn't just write about alcohol, he traded in it and had a wine press in Athafit in Yemen where he used locally grown grapes. He describes Athafit:

> *My heart is filled with love for Athafit, for its vines, and for its press.*

---

15 Boustany, Fouad Ephrem. Al-Rawaeh.

On wine, he says:

> *I drank a glass with pleasure ... then I drank another to remedy the effects of the first*
> *Let the others know that I am a man ... who experiences what life has to offer*
> *Like a dead man looks up at the bottom of the jug ... like the speck of dust in the eye when removed*
> *We watched the roses and the jasmin... and heard the flutes play their songs*
> *Our lutes never stopped playing ... but which of these three shall be demeaned*
> *You see the cymbals cry of sadness ... afraid they would be their next target*

THE DAWN OF ISLAM (622 AD - 750 AD)
The period from the "Hijrah" (the migration of prophet Muhammad and his followers from Mecca to Yathrib) up to the fall of the Umayyad Caliphate and the rise of the Abbasids.

Islamic law has traditionally prohibited alcohol and Quranic verses have been interpreted as banning drinking. As a result, the Rashidun caliphs (i.e. the first four caliphs) were very strict in enforcing the ban. Umar bin Khattab was even said to whip drunkards and even beat the Prophet's companion Khalid Ibn al-Walid for drinking. Nonetheless, as is usually the case, this did not deter people from drinking, even when the punishment went up to forty lashes during the reign of Umar bin Khattab. When the Umayyad dynasty rose to power, the Caliphs exhibited a tendency toward drinking themselves, notably Yazid Ibn Muawiyah, Abd al-Malik Ibn Marwan, Yazid Ibn Abd al-Malik, and al-Walid Ibn Yazid. This tendency was reflected in the behaviour of the common people, who returned to drinking as taverns opened and prospered. As the Arab conquests grew and the realm prospered, people became less and less strict in following religious norms. If the caliphs themselves were drinking, why should their subjects not as well? So, people drank, and poets wrote generously about alcohol and its effects. One such renowned poet was the Caliph al-Walid Ibn Yazid who went so far as to get drunk on top of the Kaaba. When asked about his religion, he gave this famous response:

> *You enquire about my religion ... know that it's the same as Abi Shaker*
> *We have our drinks pure and mixed ... we have them warm and cold*

Recalling a memory at a monastery, he said:

> *I wish I were now at the priest's convent ... where the drinks flow and songs fill the air*
> *As the bottle turns our heads turn with it ... to see us, you'd think we were mad*

Hassan Ibn Thabit

Hassan Ibn Thabit is a famous poet who witnessed the transition from the Age of Ignorance to Islam. His father was a nobleman from Yathrib[16] who converted to Islam after the Hijrah. At the time, the Prophet was in desperate need of support and was able to find it among the people of Yathrib. They offered money and men to support the tribe of Quraysh and other Arab tribes. These supporters were known as al-Ansar (The Helpers). Hassan Ibn Thabit himself was an alcoholic who enjoyed singing and worldly pleasures. His love of alcohol did not preclude him from praising the Prophet, and he was known to listen to music even in the

---

16 The ancient name of Medina

presence of the Prophet. When he spoke of alcohol in his poetry, it was always with pride, praise, and wisdom. Later in life however, he came to view his pleasure-living past with regret.

> *It is aged in the taverns for aeons ... one year after the other*
> *We drink it pure and mixed ... then listen to singing in the houses of marble*
> *It goes through your body gently ... like ants crawling on soft dry sand*
> *One glass, and if an old man has five ... you see him become young again*
> *I choose the wine of Beisan ... its soothing qualities soften my bones*

We can also see his views on life through the verses he wrote about wine:

> *I held my head, aching from wine ... and I called on him. Though defeated,*
> *He helped me when he awoke and rested and I said: ... "Life and death are one and the same!*
> *Drink wine today wherever you find it ... and know that anything good in life is temporary*[17]*."*

---

17 Boustany, Fouad Ephrem. Al-Rawaeh

Al-Akhtal

Al-Akhtal is incontestably known as the foremost poet of the Umayyad dynasty. He drank to keep warm; he drank to forget his worries; he drank to get inspired; and he drank to enhance his voice as he recited his poetry. He saw in alcohol a physical and mental remedy, and often recommended it to his followers.

Drinking did not weaken his mind, even though he occasionally liked to think of himself as, "the Prince of the Caliph" in reference to his relationship with the caliph Abd al-Malik Ibn Marwan. The latter often tried to convert al-Akhtal, a Christian, to Islam by asking him, "Why don't you convert?" It was never quite clear whether this question was serious.

Al-Akhtal was known to be protective of his religion and tried to get out of this situation by joking, and said:

> *I will, as long as you allow me to drink wine and exempt me from fasting during Ramadan.*

Abd-al Malik, whose proposal was seemingly serious, replied, "Once you become a Muslim, if you neglect the obligations of Islam, I'll break your neck."

Al-Akhtal, wagering on the Caliph's lenience, answered that he would not be seen fasting, making sacrifices, praying or going on Muslim pilgrimage, but rather intended to keep drinking and attending mass at dawn:

No! I will never observe the fast of Ramadan, nor eat the flesh of sacrifices.
Never will I drive a young and robust camel towards the valley of Mecca in the time of pilgrimage.
Never will I cry out like a donkey, "Come! To prayer!"
But I will continue to drink and prostrate myself at daybreak[18].

The caliph was not angry, but asked, "What attraction has this drink for you?"

"Sire," replied Akhtal, "When I drink, I don't worry about you any more than about the strap of my sandal."[19]

"Improvise some verses on this thought," said the caliph, "or I will break your neck"

The poet said,

If my wish makes me take two go's to empty three cups of a generous vintage,
I get up, dragging the folds of my robe as if I was your master, O Master of the Faithful. (20)

In a poem al-Akhtal recited after he and his companions sobered up from three days of drinking - only to then drink again – he said:

---

18 http://www.roger-pearse.com/weblog/2016/09/27/al-aktal-on-halal-food/. The author has made a small modification in translated version.
19 Ibid
20 Ibid

We said to the server: bring us more of yesterday's wine.
Yesterday was a better day.
He brought the jug and within it, as red as Mars,
The drink looked pure with a light foam
It was sweet perfumed water, and the glass was passed around
As its drinker dies and is brought back to life
Its death is sweet and the life it gives is sweeter

THE ABBASID PERIOD (750 AD - 1258 AD)
From the establishment of the Abbasid dynasty in 750 AD through to the Mongol invasion of Baghdad by Hülagü (Genghis Khan's grandson, and a brother of Kublai Khan) in 1258 AD.

After the fall of the Umayyad dynasty and its capital Damascus, the Abbasid dynasty rose in Baghdad. The population under the Abbasid Empire was made up of not only Arabs, but also of Persians and other ethnicities that lived in Iraq, including Christians and non-Christians.

The Abbasid caliphs sought to benefit from this diversity and gave their non-Arab subjects freedom to think and express themselves. While this freedom proved its worth in most cases, it did have its side effects such as partying, drinking, libertinism, and heresy. Alcohol played an essential part in this depraved lifestyle.

As Waliba Ibn al-Habbab, Abu Nuwas' mentor and Kufa's infamous poet put it:

> *What is the use of drinking without debauchery ... followed by adultery and sodomy.*

During the time, a disagreement arose between scholars in Hejaz (a region in the west of present-day Saudi Arabia) and those in Iraq about the prohibition of alcohol. People were able to profit from this dispute by following the Iraqi school on drinking and the Hejazi school on singing. According to Abu Nuwas:

> *His opinion on music is Hejazi ... and his opinion on drinking is Iraqi.*

This said, those who did drink did not actually need scholars to justify their behaviour. As Ibn Masud and Abu Hanifa said, these people drank regardless of the drink's prohibition. Part of the pleasure they got from the drink was from the very fact that it was outlawed. As Abu Nuwas said:

> *If they say it is forbidden, then forbidden it is ... but there is sweet pleasure in the outlawed.*

Alcohol gained popularity after the caliphs started drinking and hosting entertainment gatherings at their palaces; beautiful women sang, and handsome young men went around offering guests alcohol, drinking and much more... Ibn al-Mu'tazz described one of the Caliph al-Amin's gatherings, "A drink with the colour of saffron was served. It was purer that a lover's embrace and smelled sweeter. Servers as radiant as a full moon went around with glasses twinkling like stars. They served the guests as the maids appeared from behind the curtains holding pitchers. Everyone drank from dawn till dusk. He then ordered 10,000 dinars to be brought on trays. When they were, he had them scattered as the guests hurried to get their share."

Baghdad and neighbouring towns were filled with taverns and abbeys where both Arabs and non-Arabs ("Ajam") met.

The abbeys had their own taverns and gardens away from the places of worship, and on Sundays and religious holidays, they were filled with those who sought the wine drunk by Christians. As Abu Nuwas said:

If the religion of the Prophet Mohamed prohibits it …
follow the religion of Christ when you drink.

Abbasid poets wrote many verses praising wine and describing wine drinkers, their debauchery, servants, and maids. Their poems continue to have significant literary merit and were some of the most beautiful poems written at the time. Their verses reflected their kind and gentle spirits, and the age of prosperity and indulgence they lived in.

Abu Nuwas (762 AD – 814 AD)
Alcohol and revelry

Al-Hasan Ibn Hani, known as Abu Nuwas, was the grandson of the governor of Khorasan and the son of a solider in Marwan Ibn Mohammed's army. His father was an Arab from Damascus and his mother was a Persian from Ahvaz. He was born in Ahvaz but his mother moved him to Basra at the age of two.

He first worked as an assistant for hire at parties where he would carry supplies and stay until the party ended. The dissolute poet from Kufa Waliba Ibn al-Habbab once heard him playing the oud and was fascinated by him. He later became his mentor and took him to Kufa where he taught him poetry. After his stay in Kufa, at the age of 30, Abu Nuwas travelled to Baghdad, the capital of Harun al-Rashid's caliphate. Here, he got the opportunity to meet the caliph, who liked the young poet and offered him his support. This included turning a blind eye to the poet's bad habits, drinking, and his mockery of religion and pardoning his many offences. The poet was often in the company of miscreants who gathered at the banks of the Sarat canal in Baghdad to exchange poetry and drink wine. Given his lifestyle, Abu Nuwas never became an official court poet to the caliph, as Harun al-Rashid was determined to preserve the stability and integrity of the caliphate.

Abu Nuwas showed very promising talent at a young age. One of his early verses talked of love:

A man in love is burdened with desire ... and is weakened by the joy he feels.

He memorized the Qur'an, and had knowledge of Greek and Indian philosophy, so much so that he was known as "the most learned man in Basra". It was said that "the least of Abu Nuwas' skills was poetry."

However, the true Abu Nuwas, his truth and his soul, are revealed in his poetry, but not his serious verses, rather in his praise of wine and revelry. The latter clearly reflect the poet's true desires.

Abu Nuwas drank. He was devoted to drinking and to

praising alcohol. In fact, his innovation in describing the fermented drinks made his poems stand out as genres of their own and dominated his poetic oeuvre. He used adjectives of beauty and tenderness to describe the glasses, the gatherings, the servers, the drinking sessions, etc. His descriptions were clear and straightforward, never concealed, and sought to understand all the pleasurable experiences of drinking.

> *Ho! a cup, and fill it up, and tell me it is wine,*
> *For never will I drink in shade if I can drink in shine.*
> *Curst and poor is every hour that sober I must go,*
> *But rich am I whene'er well drunk I stagger to and fro.*[21]

On revelry:

> *The young moves from one drunken state to another ...*
> *and as time passes, he moves to the castle of eternity .*

And he refused to be blamed for his worship of wine:

> *Leave off blaming me, for blame is temptation,*
> *And medicate me with what had been my malady.*
> *A golden wine, that sorrows never visit,*
> *Were a stone to touch it that stone would be touched by joy.*
> *As she stood with her wine jar in the dark of the night,*

---

21 Reynold A. Nicholson, Translations of Eastern Poetry and Prose (Cambridge at the University Press, 1922), no. 33.

The bright light of her face illuminated the house.
From the mouth of the jar she dispatched a wine so pure,
That to sieve it with the eye was to lose consciousness.
So refined that water did not suit it
In fineness and recoiled from its form.
Were you to mix it with light they would blend
And give birth to multiple lights. [22]

He drank from dawn and his poems have become the most comprehensive inventory of taverns and pleasure gardens in Baghdad and outside the city. Every place he visited and every drink he had was described in his verses,

The wretched looked for ruins to lament ... I looked for the neighbourhood's taverns to frequent.

As for those who disapproved of his lifestyle, he encouraged them to join him rather than criticise him:

Drink and be generous with all that you possess ... Don't hoard a thing today fearing poverty tomorrow
You who reproach me, your message has reached me ... Though I do pardon it, do not repeat it
Were it meant as advice, I would accept it ... But your blame is based on envy instead.

---

22 Ewald Wagner, Abu Nuwas.

His poems on wine, known as al-Khamriyat, draw the portrait of a revolutionary man who rejected the old. He was a man of the people, who leaned more toward the Persian culture than the Arabic one. He disliked the Bedouin lifestyle and disdained the Jahiliyya poets with their whining verses about love. He criticized these Arab poets while praising the pleasures of drinking:

> *Don't cry for Layla and don't rejoice over Hind*
> *Instead, drink to the rose from a rosy red wine.*
> *A glass which, when tipped down the drinker's throat,*
> *Leaves its redness in both the eye and the cheek.*
> *For the wine is a ruby and the goblet a pearl,*
> *From the hand of a slim-figured maiden.*
> *She pours out one draught for you from her eye and from her hand…*
> *Yet another, 'til you cannot escape growing doubly drunk.*
> *My companions have but one opiate, while I have two*
> *By such a thing, I alone have been favoured.*[23]

Abu Nuwas' only true faith was pleasure. His beliefs and his actions were all based on his desires, for the sake of which he was prepared to forgo religion and norms. For him, a life filled with wine and love was worth eternal damnation:

---

23 https://www.princeton.edu/~arabic/poetry/layla.html

> *You who reproach the pure red draught ... go to heaven and leave me to the fire.*

He found his time too precious to spend praying, instead, whenever he heard the call to prayer, he would say to his server:

> *Give me a cup to distract from the muezzin's call.*

During Ramadan, after the fasting he was coerced into would get too overwhelming, he would abandon the fast and instead drank to excess. His excuse was rather philosophical,

> *Would forgiveness have been created save for the sinful man?*

If he did ever ask for forgiveness, he didn't fail to defend his love of alcohol:

> *Place the bottle aside ... and with it the holy book*
> *Take three sips from the first ... and read a few verses from the second*
> *While one is evil, the other is good ... and so on balance God forgives my sins.*

It is important to note however that Abu Nuwas was neither a heretic nor an atheist. He was liberal in religious practices and preferred to wager on God's forgiveness for his revelries and obscenities. Towards the end of his life, he had had his fill of excesses and adopted a quieter lifestyle.

Omar Khayyam (1042 AD – 1131 AD)
While you live, drink!

Omar Ibn Ibrahim Khayyam was born in 1042AD in Nishapur (the capital of the province of Khorasan in present day Iran), then a centre for knowledge and learning. He was a thinker, a poet, an astronomer, and a mathematician. His fame was initially limited to his scientific achievements, and the Western world did not discover his poetic genius until 730 years after his death (in Nishapur in 1131) when the English writer Edward Fitzgerald translated his works from Persian into English. Khayyam's poems, known as al-Rubaiyyat, are short poems discrete in form and content. Ten years after Fitzgerald's death, a club dedicated to the Persian poet was established in London with the mission of preserving Khayyam's poems. The club even wrote to the Shah of Iran asking him to maintain and beautify the late poet's tomb.

The most frequently-recurring words in Khayyam's poetry are terms like wine, tavern, server, jug, oud, flute, singer, etc. The most dominant themes are life passing and the need to take advantage of it while alive, and the inability of Man to know where he comes from or where he is going. His poems often encouraged others to enjoy the limited days they have on earth, and to accept things as they are since, as humans, we can't possess all the knowledge.

If his philosophy could be summed up in one expression, it would be; you cannot change the past, and you cannot tell what tomorrow may bring, so seize the opportunities of today and enjoy them.

In his own words,

> *Ah! my Beloved, fill the Cup that clears*
> *To-day of past Regrets and future Fears*
> *To-morrow?--Why, To-morrow I may be*
> *Myself with Yesterday's Sev'n Thousand Years.*
> ...
> *And if the Cup you drink, the Lip you press,*
> *End in what All begins and ends in—Yes;*
> *Imagine then you are what heretofore*
> *You were—hereafter you shall not be less.*
> ...
> *Waste not your Hour, nor in the vain pursuit*
> *Of This and That endeavour and dispute;*
> *Better be merry with the fruitful Grape*
> *Than sadden after none, or bitter, Fruit.*[24]

Scholars had trouble understanding Omar Khayyam. Some thought that he was mocking religion, especially as he advocated drinking all days of the week:

> *Ye, who cease not to drink on common days,*
> *Do not on Friday quit your drinking ways;*
> *Adopt my creed, and count all days the same,*

---

24 Rubaiyat of Omar Khayyam, Translated by Edward Fitzgerald, Second edition, 1868

Be worshippers of God, and not of days.

He may have been referencing Christ: "the Sabbath was made for man, not man for the Sabbath".

For Ramadan, he wished he could remain unconscious throughout the month, so he wouldn't have to bear separation from wine,

> *They say that the moon of Ramazan shines out again*
> *Henceforth one cannot linger over the wine;*
> *At the end of Sha'ban I will drink so much wine*
> *That during Ramazan I may be found drunk until the festival (arrives).*

He preferred a glass in his hand to rolling out the prayer mat:

> *To the wine-house I saw the sage repair,*
> *Bearing a wine-cup, and a mat for prayer;*
> *I said, «O Shaikh, what does this conduct mean?»*
> *Said he, «Go drink! the world is naught but air.»*

Khayyam believed that mankind was influenced by a hidden power that couldn't be controlled, and that gave him no choice between doing good and bad. He believed in fate,

> *We are no other than a moving row*

> *Of Magic Shadow-shapes that come and go*
> *Round with the Sun-illumined Lantern held*
> *In Midnight by the Master of the Show.*

He accused those sleeping of letting life's joys go to waste,

> *Dreaming when Dawn's Left Hand was in the Sky*
> *I heard a Voice within the Tavern cry,*
> *"Awake, my Little ones, and fill the Cup*
> *Before Life's Liquor in its Cup be dry."*

And encouraged his listeners to embrace love,

> *O heart! when on the Loved One's sweets you feed,*
> *You lose yourself, but find your Self indeed;*
> *And, when you drink of His entrancing cup,*
> *You hasten your escape from quick and dead!*

As for religion, he did ask for God's forgiveness at the end of his life,

> *Oh! Thou who knowest the secrets of the hearts of all,*
> *Protector of all in their hours of helplessness:*
> *Oh, Lord! grant me repentance and accept my excuses,*
> *Oh! Thou who grantest repentance and acceptest the excuses of all.* [25]

---

25 https://www.gutenberg.org/files/38511/38511-h/38511-h.htm#FNanchor_83_83

Ibn al-Farid (1162 AD – 1234 AD)

Ibn al-Farid is a Sufi poet nicknamed the "sultan of lovers". His poetry was mystical and spiritual. Although his family origins lay in Hama in Syria, Ibn Farid was in fact born in Cairo in 1162 AD and died there in 1234 AD. He grew up in a devout and virtuous home, and adopted Sufism early on in his life. He went on spiritual retreats to abandoned mosques, the Mokattam hills, and a valley known as the Oasis of the Wretches (Wadi al-Mustad'afin). He went to Mecca where he stayed for 15 years, retreated in a valley, and developed his poetic skills. He then returned to Egypt when the country was under the rule of the Ayyubid dynasty.

He was a sociable, kind, gentle, and eloquent person. He was often fascinated by beauty - to the point of distress - and found beauty in everything from nature to music. When he heard a tune he liked, he would dance right then and there. It is said that he had maidens who would play music and sing for him while he danced. His son recalled a story of how his father was walking in the souk in Cairo when he passed by a group of people singing. As soon as he heard the music, he shouted and started dancing in the middle of the market. People joined, and the crowd grew until most of them fell to the floor. Ibn Farid then took his clothes off and threw them to the crowd, only to be carried away to al-Azhar mosque half naked.

Ibn al-Farid's most famous poem is the Ode to Wine, an important Sufi meditation on the drink. Wine in Sufi poems was considered a symbol of drunkenness and ecstasy, and referred to inebriation in the love of God and ecstasy in unity with Him.

> *In memory of the Beloved*
> *We drank a wine;*
> *Intoxicated we were*
> *With the wine before*
> *It was created.*

> *The full moon is its cup*
> *And it is the brightest Sun.*
> *Crescent Moon passes it around*
> *And stars appear*
> *As it is diluted for the drinkers.*

After placing wine along with the stars, he attributes magical powers to it compared with the miracles of Christ,

> *And in the shade of its vineyard,*
> *If they were to lie,*
> *The sick who were cureless*
> *Would rise cured.*

> *Were someone lame brought*
> *Near to its dwelling place,*
> *He would walk*
> *And the mute talk*
> *By its flavour's grace.*

*And were it poured
Onto a grave,
The dead would rise
Full of spirit, revived.*

*Were its perfume to spread
Eastward, and the deprived
Were in the West,
They too would feel its
Fragrance in their midst.*

He further describes the drink,

*They say to me, 'Describe this wine
For you know its qualities divine.'
And I say yes
I do have knowledge of this wine!
It's clear, but not of water.
It's weightless, soft, but not of air.
It's luminous, but not of fie.
It's a spirit without body!*

He envied monks for their ability to drink it,

*They say to me,
'You have drunk the sin.'
I say, 'Never! I have drunk
That which it would be a sin*

Not to drink'

Happy are the convent dwellers
Intoxicated by it so often, yet
They drank it not!
But their aspired to the heights!

I felt its intoxication
When still a child,
And it will remain with me
Though my bones may decay.

The poem's final verses are reminiscent of Omar Khayyam's view on eternity:

Were you drunk with it
For an hour and no more
You would feel the world your slave
To rule and command, and you its king.

There is no happiness in this world
To him who lives sober,
And one who does not die drunk with it
Will miss the benefit of fulfilment.[26]

---

26 Jamal, Mahmood. Islamic Mystical Poetry: Sufi Verse from the early Mystics to Rumi, Penguin UK, Oct 29, 2009

ix

The Milk of Lions - A History of Alcohol in the Middle East

(Above) Christ's last supper with his disciples, a glass of wine placed in front of him, distributing bread as a symbol of his own body - symbolically reenacted by priests the world over to this day.

(Above) Jesus Christ in front of the jars of water he turned to wine, *(left)*.

(Previous page) Queen Esther kicking the evil Haman out. Painting by Arthur A. Dixon.

(Above) Jerusalem sits at the heart of Abrahamic religions. The Dome of the Rock is shown here photographed behind barbed wire.

(Below) The Ka'baah, a building located in the centre of the Sacred Mosque in Mecca, Saudi Arabia, shown here in a rare photograph published in 1925.

The Milk of Lions - A History of Alcohol in the Middle East

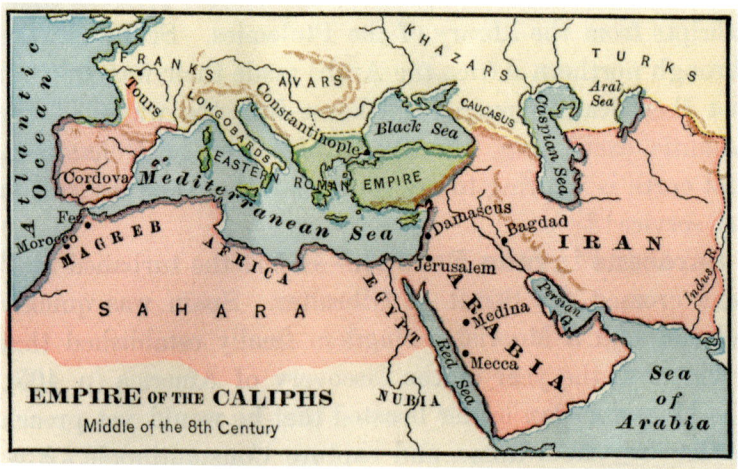

(Above) The empire of the Rashidun caliphs (in red), mid-eighth century.

(Left) Painting of the Uzbek leader Tamerlane who invaded most of Asia Minor.

(Opposite top) The Mosque of Cordoba is a symbol of Arab culture in Andalousia.

(Opposite bottom) Al-A'sha…or the Damp Grave.

The Milk of Lions - A History of Alcohol in the Middle East

(Above and Opposite) Illustrations representing Omar Khayyam's view on life included in the English edition of his Rubaiyyat publishrd in 1959.

Ah, fill the cup: what boots it to repeat
How Time is slipping underneath our feet:
Unborn To-morrow, and dead Yesterday
Why fret about them if To-day be sweet.

OMAR KHAYYÁM

The Milk of Lions - A History of Alcohol in the Middle East

(Top) A 19th century watercolour depicts Napoleon paying final tribute to the Sphynx at Giza, Egypt.

(Below left) A monument in Cairo to Ahmad Shawqy, Egyptian Prince of Poets.

(Below centre) Hafez-Ibrahim, Poet of the Nile.

(Below right) Bechara al-Khoury (Al Akhtal as-Saghir).

THE ANDALUSIAN PERIOD
Tariq Ibn Ziyad's invasion of Andalusia in 710 AD, through to the fall of Granada in 1492 AD.

Before the Arab conquest, Spain was in political and social turmoil. Tariq Ibn Ziyad invaded southern Spain with an army of 7,000 Berber and 300 Arab soldiers. As the Arabs settled in Andalusia, they brought with them their poetry. Their Umayyad style was influenced by the beautiful nature of Spain, its songs, and its lively spirit. Berbers and Arabs, now living alongside Christians, adopted Christian romantic poetry, which often mentions churches, priests and crosses. As for wine, they drank it because they loved it, and loved gatherings where they could drink, sing, and reference the words of Abu Nuwas.

She pours you wine from her eye, and from her hand ... Wine until you are twice drunk without escape.

And the words of Ibn Abd Rabbih:

She handed me the glass and enchanted me with her look ... As she poured the wine, I drank from her eyes before her hands.

Drinking sessions in the Andalusian period were infamous for their obscenities, revelry, and violation of religious rules. The servants were often subject to advances, like Ibn Khafaja's description of a humped black server:

> *His skin got darker ... and the wine redder*
> *Like coal burning ... and a flaming fire.*

The art of poetry grew and diversified, the Andalusians developed their own style called the *Muwashshah*. The poetic form was developed for singing and to bring a sublime musical genre to Spain that was rather poor in this regard before the Arab conquest. After the Arabs settled in the area, they promoted their music and poetry, and the *Muwashahah* became popular fixtures at musical gatherings. The lifestyle in Andalusia was one of entertainment, pleasure, music, and poetry. Singers were admired, and the most popular songs spoke of love, wine, and the beauty of Andalusia. An example is Ibn al-Khatib's comparison of wine to a guide leading the way to the right path:

> *On nights that keep lovers' secrets ... perils come with the rising sun.*
> *Glasses sparkle like stars ... guiding love's joyous path.*
> *A night with no imperfections ... save how fast it can pass.*

It was said complaints should be addressed to servants and not to judges:

> *Cupbearer, to you I bring my sorrows ... Even if my calls remain ignored.*

The song continues:

I wandered lost in his beauty
And drank wine as he rested
Whenever he awoke from his drunken state
He drew the bottle closer, reclined,
And poured me four more glasses.

THE MAMLUK AND OTTOMAN PERIOD
Hülagü's invasion of Baghdad in 1258 AD through to Napoleon I's conquest of Egypt in 1798 AD.

When the Mongols invaded Iraq and the Levant, they wreaked havoc in the region, killed, vandalised, and spread terror. People had no time to forget Hülagü's atrocities in Baghdad before Tamerlane headed for the Levant in 1400 AD, destroying Aleppo, Homs, Hama, Baalbek and Damascus. His army killed whoever stood in their way, burned the Umayyad mosque in Damascus and many other places of worship, and schools, raped women, stomped over children with their horses, and took over monasteries on the coasts of Egypt and Greater Syria. This was the state the region was in at the time. Things were no better in the Arabian Peninsula or the Maghreb. Rulers were regularly deposed and changed, and Muslims were fleeing from the Spanish in Andalusia. During these dire times, the Ottomans were able to prosper and conquer Constantinople in 1453 AD. They set up their empire with Istanbul as its capital, and expanded it throughout the Arab world. They took Greater Syria and Egypt from the Mamluks and deposed Al-Mutawakkil, the Abbasid caliph. The guardianship of the two holy mosques was in the Ottomans' hands, and for the first time, it was in the hands of non-Arabs and men outside the tribe of Quraysh. From Egypt and Greater Syria, the Ottomans expanded their empire to Iraq, the Arabian Peninsula, Yemen, Tunis, and Algeria.

However, the Ottoman period was filled with terror and corruption. Scientists were killed, books destroyed, and schools suppressed. It was a time of injustice, prohibitions, and oppressions. The liberal days of Andalusia were long gone, along with the drinking sessions of Baghdad and Kufa. The Ottoman rulers tried to limit entertainment, singing, and drinking.

Poetry suffered, as did poets, and people grew more religious. Poems that were written praised the Prophet and asked for his mercy. This trend was also adopted by Arab Christians who wrote poems about Christ and his disciples.

Wine and alcohol were no longer popular subjects. Soirées were no longer held at the caliphs' and princes' palaces. Taverns closed, and rulers governed with an iron fist, and imposed islamic law firmly.

The only exception in terms of alcohol was made for monasteries and Christian houses of worship. Christians were allowed to produce wine to practice their religious rites. This made wine-making the "speciality" of Christians. Thanks to their connections with the West, monasteries were able to stay up to date with developments in the industry. They were the first to import modern equipment and the first printing press in the Near East. Wine production became widespread among Christians, and as the produce became increasingly difficult to store, producers in mountainous regions started distilling the fermented liquids into araq. The months of October and November (*tisherin* in Arabic) were the season for making araq, and villagers would compete on who got to use the traditional still called the *karaki*, only available at monasteries or in the houses of the elite.

RENAISSANCE
Napoleon's invasion of Egypt in 1798 AD through to the middle of the 20th century.

When Napoleon invaded Egypt, it was debilitated, and in a state of chaos and ignorance. He pushed the Ottomans to Upper Egypt and hoped to block England's path to India. He launched social reforms and education campaigns to gain the trust of the Egyptians, and brought scientists, engineers, doctors, and industrialists to establish factories, observatories, clubs, libraries, and gardens. The Egyptians were amazed by the French culture they were exposed to, even though the French did not stay long. Napoleon was obliged to hand over Egypt to the Ottoman leader Mohammed Ali, and Egyptians swore allegiance to the latter in 1805 AD. Ali, having witnessed the reform and development achievements of the French, decided to seek help from Europe, especially the French, to launch similar development projects. Thanks to his efforts, Egypt built a closer relationship with the West. In 1882 AD, England, the Ottoman Empire's ally, took control of the Suez Canal while Mohammed Ali's heirs remained the nominal rulers. Egypt's openness to the West, its religious diversity, and its economic and touristic significance, earned it the name "Mother of the World" (*Umm al-Dunya*). Arab and foreign immigrants flocked to Cairo. Egyptians, with their famous joie de vivre, adapted well to the Western lifestyle. The arts flourished, and entertainment clubs multiplied as Cairo became the capital of the East and Alexandria its aristocratic centre. Alcohol was available to all social classes, and was consumed widely. Palaces and villas nearly always included a private bar stocked with all sorts of spirits and drinks.

Two poets gained special fame during this time: Hafez Ibrahim, dubbed the "Poet of the Nile", and Ahmed Shawqi, dubbed "the Prince of Poets".

Hafez Ibrahim, the Poet of the Nile (1872 – 1932)

Hafez Ibrahim was born on a ship docked on the banks of the Nile in the governorate of Asyut. He was born to an Egyptian father and a Turkish mother, and worked for the lawyer Mohammed Abu Shadi, one of the leaders of the 1919 revolution. He later enlisted in the military academy and was sent to Sudan during the Egyptian campaign there. He became a distinguished and renowned man not only for his poetry skills but also for his incredible memory. In fact, his poems often constituted a record of important events in the history of Egypt. This history included alcohol,

> *This darkness has awoken my sickness ... cupbearer bring me some wine*
> *In a glass, a cup, or both ... or bring the jug for my remedy*
> *If it weren't for piety, why then is it banned ... why did our ancestors pray intoxicated*
> *Even after the wise verses were revealed ... and the matter cleared*

He likened the colour of wine to the rosy cheeks of a blushing bride:

Cupbearer pour the wine ... until we could only whisper and hardly speak
They say the grapes were pressed ... from the cheeks of beauties on their wedding day .

In a poem addressed to some of his friends in Sudan, he reminded them of his status as the "Imam of the intoxicated".

Those gathered for wine are the best of drinkers ... they bring back with it ancient years
Remember me with glasses in your hands ... remember me as the Imam of the intoxicated.

Ahmed Shawqi, the Prince of Poets (1869-1932)

Ahmed Shawqi was born in Cairo to a Kurdish family. He studied law and French literature. He was then offered a job in the court of the Khedive Abbas II, where he became an influential figure. After World War I, the English overthrew the court of the Khedive due to its connection with the Ottomans, and Shawqi was exiled to Andalusia. After the war ended, he returned to Egypt in 1919 where he spent the rest of his life writing.

His most famous poem about wine is called Ramadan is Over, and describes how he misses wine during the month of Ramadan.

Ramadan is over… cupbearer, bring me the wine
I long for my beloved and it longs for me
How much I used to spend in her presence
How little time I spent obeying the Creator
God forgives all evils and sins
And from sinning I have found no protection
Yesterday obedience was my prison
Today the Eid has set me free
She smiled at me with happiness
The daughter of the vine has honour still
Pour my drink free of reprimand
And stay until the cockerel sings
Pure light shines as if from her cheeks
Red and yellow rays sparkle in glasses
Each a different woman
Each a different beauty
Cupbearer don't spill her blood
The blood of lovers is spilled enough
Don't return with the glass unless full
For worries and troubles fill my soul
Perhaps with wine and its mighty power
I can escape this world of hypocrisy.

Arabian Peninsula

In the Arabian Peninsula, the first Saudi state (1714-1818) was religiously conservative as it was built on an alliance between Sheikh Mohammed Ibn Abd al-Wahhab, who founded the religious movement now called Wahhabism, and Mohammed Ibn Saud. However, Ottoman forces gained control of the land after a series of wars, and internal conflicts continued ravaging the peninsula (either between local tribes or with the Ottomans) until 1902 when Abdulaziz Ibn Abdul Rahman Al Saud founded the modern Saudi State. In this new country, the entire territory was considered holy. The shahada or Islamic declaration of faith was inscribed on the national flag attesting to the country's adherence to Wahhabism, the strictest and most conservative sect in Sunni Islam. In this environment, alcohol was strictly prohibited and there were harsh punishments for consumers or producers of alcohol. These rules still apply today to anyone living in Saudi Arabia.

On the coast of what is now known as the United Arab Emirates, Great Britain sought to beat its rivals France and Holland in gaining control of the territory to secure a trading route and its interests in India and East Asia. The population of the country in the 1950s was no more than 70,000 people, most of whom were Sunni Muslims. They were practicing and devoted Muslims but were also tolerant of expatriates who settled in their land and allowed them to drink alcohol.

Iraq

Iraq, like other Arab countries, was also subject to Ottoman rule. Baghdad was ruled by Midhat Pasha (1869-1872) who had previously been a governor of the Danube Province. There, he was exposed to, and gained experience in, architecture, culture, and science. Similar to Mohammed Ali's development campaign in Egypt, Midhat Pasha developed Baghdad through projects he undertook with the support of Western nations, mainly Great Britain. One of his most important accomplishment was rolling out a land ownership system that helped reduce the number of nomads in Iraq by almost half.

The Levant

The Levant region was divided into five provinces in 1877: Aleppo, Deir Ezzor, Beirut, Damascus, and the Mount Lebanon Mutasarrifate. However, after the end of World War I and the fall of the Ottoman Empire, the borders were reshaped radically. Iraq, Jordan and Palestine were put under English rule while France governed Lebanon and Syria. During the reign of the Ottomans, who emphasised their status as the legitimate caliphs and rulers of the Muslim world, alcohol was not regulated. Christians were allowed to produce alcoholic drinks, which were made available to everyone, even Muslims. In fact, thanks to Turkey's historical interactions with the West, the Ottomans were more tolerant when it came to alcohol. Furthermore, they had their own traditional drink called raki, a type of spirit very similar to the Levantine araq and the Greek ouzo. Its origins can be traced back to the tsipuro spirit that was traditionally distilled by Orthodox monks living in the holy Mount Athos in northern Greece in the 14th century.

In his memoir, Elie Touma[27], a Lebanese public servant, recalls a story that highlights the Ottomans' approach to alcohol.

It was said that Jamal Pasha, the Ottoman military leader appointed as Governor of Greater Syria in 1915 and known as "the butcher", only had one punishment for all types of offenses: death by hanging. Whether the person was guilty of murder or stealing a loaf of bread to feed his children, he would be hanged. Jamal Pasha ruled from Alay in Mount Lebanon and was very fond of araq. He would often call some of the locals to join him for a drink, including a man called Melhem al-Boustani from the town of Deir al-Qamar who managed the railway station in the city of Alay. During these gatherings, Boustani would jokingly give himself a military promotion or medal after each drink, going from a mere private soldier to general. The story goes that one time, Jamal Pasha was late to arrive. Boustani started drinking and assigning himself military ranks and awards as usual. When a messenger arrived informing him that Jamal Pasha was now ready to see him, Boustani refused to comply. The next day,

---

27 Elie Touma (1911-1998) also happens to be the author's father-in-law. He was a keen araq drinker, and the author has fond memories of drinking sessions with him.

he realized the gravity of what he had done and requested an urgent meeting with Pasha to apologise. The latter's secretary replied that the ruler was furious and that Boustani would have to wait for his punishment to be announced. Boustani then spoke to the secretary in confidence and asked him to relay the following message to Jamal Pasha, "It was late and I had had many drinks already. I looked at my shoulder and saw that I had many medals and military ranks pinned to my jacket. According to military protocol, lower ranked personnel can't summon those of a higher rank. This is why I refused to join you." When Jamal Pasha received the message, he smiled (a rarity), summoned Boustani, and told him, "The medals and ranks on my shoulder are real while the ones on yours are not" …. Boustani was then forgiven.

Bechara al-Khoury (Al Akhtal as-Saghir) (1885 - 1968)

Wisdom has taught us with age
To live intoxicated
So bring over the glasses and the music

Bechara al-Khoury was born in Beirut in 1885 and died in 1968. He was known as Al Akhtal as-Saghir (i.e. Al Akhtal the Small), his pen name from the start of his literary career. He studied with Gibran Khalil Gibran at the Collège de La Sagesse and later became Chairman of the Journalists Union. During the Ottoman occupation of Lebanon, his writings and poems often called for freedom and revolution. As for alcohol, his most famous poem is entitled The Etiquette of Drinking:

> *I found enchantment in beauty and revolution in cups*
> *I dyed stories of love with the blood from my wounds*
> *Love and wine were born on my birthday*
> *And shall keep me company until my dying day*
> *You who slaughtered the grapes*
> *Your hands red with their blood*
> *Blessings come with your butchery*
> *If you gather for a drink, keep away*
> *Idleness of love and drink*
> *The etiquette of drinking requires*
> *That you remain intoxicated*
> *As long as the wine flows*
> *How I long to drink from that spring*
> *I have no thirst for clear water*
> *I wish time would take me back*
> *To bright red wine*
> *And clear night skies*
> *I drink from their souls and give them mine*
> *And surrender my night to dawn*

After praising the pleasures wine brings, he ends his poem with a comment on life,

> *There are those who let life slip away*
> *Me, my life, I hold tight and dear*
> *For every sunset I make a sacrifice*
> *For a new sun to be born again*

The Maghreb

After the fall of the Ottoman Empire, Algeria, Tunisia and Morocco were placed under French rule. This Western occupation, compounded with the region's geographic proximity to Europe, meant that alcohol was widely available. No laws were passed to prohibit alcohol, and no one would stop a Muslim from drinking. However, drinking remained rare in these communities due to family and religious pressures, and a desire to firmly reject the culture of the occupiers.

CHAPTER IV

Alcohol in Lebanon

Excellent Wine from the Highest Peaks
Who Invented Araq?
What is Aniseed?
The Production of Araq
Alcohol Content
Araq and the Law
Araq and the Community
Sayings and Proverbs Related to Alcohol

EXCELLENT WINE FROM THE HIGHEST PEAKS

One of the oldest references to alcohol in the Fertile Crescent comes from the ancient kingdom of Ugarit. It dates back to 7,500 BC and was discovered at the Ras Shamra archaeological site, 12 kilometres away from Latakia on the coast of modern Syria. Ugarit had its own alphabet, one of the most comprehensive and richest among ancient civilisations, and invented the first alphabet (as opposed to writing system) in the world. In one famous epic written about the city, the god El, considered as the god among all deities, summoned the Rephaites (the judges and the virtuous) to his temple to announce the crowning of his son Baal. The temple servants sacrificed the animals and held a feast to celebrate. They ate and drank for six days. The text of the epic reads:

> *Sweet wine from Suraneme[28], Wine from the land of springs,*
> *Excellent wine from the highest peaks of Lebanon,*
> *Irrigated by the dew and cultivated by El.*
> *The day passed then another as the Rephaites ate and drank.*
> *A third day, a fourth day, a fifth day, and a sixth.*
> *The Rephaites still ate and drank*
> *In the house of hospitality*

---

28 Possibly the name of a region

From the fruit harvested from the heart of Lebanon.[29]

The area now known as Lebanon has always been known for its fertile vineyards and the quality of its wine. Seven centuries after the Ugarit text was written, another testimony was made to Lebanon's wine by the Biblical prophet Hosea who wrote on forgiveness:

> *I will be as the dew unto Israel,*
> *He shall grow as the lily*
> *And cast forth his roots as Lebanon*
> *… His branches shall spread,*
> *And his beauty shall be as the olive tree,*
> *and his smell as Lebanon.*
> *They that dwell under his shadow shall return,*
> *they shall revive as the corn,*
> *and grow as the vine,*
> *the scent thereof shall be as the wine of Lebanon.*[30]

More recently, Dominique Pieri who headed the French archaeological expedition that excavated downtown Beirut, wrote about the wine trade in the Byzantine Empire (4th to 7th centuries). He said that the few texts that do mention wine presses in the East clearly indicate which producers and products were best. At the time, only the noble and wealthy

---

29 Khoury Harb, Antoine. Lebanon, the Name and the Entity over 4,000 years, Lebanese Heirtage Foundation. Freiha, Anis. Epics and Legends, Virolleaud. Les Rephaim.
30 Hosea 14:5-9

of Gaul could afford them. These included people like King Eberulf or a noble woman known for donating wine made in Gaza, Palestine to her church in Lyon every day. No feast was complete without these products that were highly coveted by the nobles, courts, and emperors.

When Justin II was crowned emperor, the celebration feast only included wine imported from the East. This wine most likely found its way to the Byzantine Empire through the clergy who had connections with religious communities and monks in the East. They imported it, stored it to use in the rite of communion, and traded in it for very high prices.

The religious communities on both shores of the Mediterranean shared strong ties. At that time, wine was available across the near and middle east. After the birth of Islam, wine making became confined to Christian communities, and especially to monasteries. These became key actors in the entire process, from the production of wine to its consumption and sale. So much so that some monasteries in Kufa in Iraq even had their own taverns. These monasteries were often built on hills and surrounded with fields and springs. They served as rest houses and shelters for travellers. Inns were rare at the time, so the rulers encouraged monasteries to take in any travelling Muslims. As for poets, they were allowed to stay and live there as they pleased and in Arabic, a new literary genre was born out of the collaboration. It was known as "monastic literature" and was the best at describing entertainment and friendly gatherings.[31]

This meant that monasteries became popular and attracted many visitors, some of whom did not come for religious reasons. The monastries owned vast plots of land and had the financial means to cultivate them, improve their crops, and produce wine. They also had the capacity to store the wine in proper conditions after pressing the grapes; wine had to be stored in cellars at a stable humidity rate (70% to 75%) and a specific temperature (12°C), and had to be kept in special barrels to prevent it from turning into vinegar, thereby risking the year's crops. Wine storage required lots of space and stringent conditions of temperature and humidity. The advent of distillation was able to change this state of affairs. Around the IXth century, chemist Jabir Ibn Hayyan perfected the distillation techniques and apparatus, which ultimately enabled the distillation of wine and other fermented alcoholic drinks. Jabir Ibn Hayyan had provided the golden solution to a storage problem: Distilled drinks could be more easily stored than wine. They required less space and only needed room temperature.

Jabir Ibn Hayyan

Who is Jabir Ibn Hayyan? Jabir Ibn Hayyan, also known in the West as Geber, is one of the greatest medieval scholars who led chemistry away from what we now call alchemy and

---

31 Esfahani, Abi Faraj, al-Diyarat, Riyad Najib al-Rayyis Press

took an approach that we would nowadays regard as more scientific. Historians disagree on his place of birth. He was born around 721 AD either in Upper Mesopotamia east of the Euphrates or in Khorasan in Iran. His father migrated to Kufa in Iraq toward the end of the Umayyad period and the start of the Abbasid dynasty. His father worked as a pharmacist and this is probably the reason behind Jabir's perusal of chemistry. He received his training in religion, language, and chemistry at the hands of Imam Jafar as-Sadiq and went on to practice medicine under the patronage of Jafar al-Barmaki, a vizier of the Arab Abbasid caliph Harun al-Rashid. When the Barmaki family fell from grace, Jabir was imprisoned and remained in a cell until his death in 815 AD.

The French chemist Marcellin Berthelot (1827-1907 AD) praised Jabir's work and said he was to chemistry what Aristotle was to logic. Jabir has in fact earned many titles, including the Father of Chemistry, Sheikh of Muslim Chemistry, and the Ultimate Professor.

Meanwhile, the lands the monasteries owned were so large and scattered that they were unable to manage them without partners. They found these partners in their parishes and encouraged them to invest in a plot of land in exchange for a share of the wine.

However, this produce was directly linked to the nature of the land and its climate. In Egypt and Iraq, most of the ethanol produced was extracted from dates and figs while in Syria, Lebanon, Palestine and Jordan, most of it was extracted from grapes. This remains true today.

Father Dr César Mourani writes about Lebanon's resources in his book, *Religious Architecture of Kobayat*[32] *at the time of the Crusaders*, "Wine making declined under the Abbasids who banned the drink. It became limited to religious communities who used basic tools that are now lost. The scarcity of caves for storage drove farmers to start distilling and making araq."

This suggests that the production of araq may have started during the Abbasid period. From 750 AD until 1258 AD, the Abbasid Caliphate was ruled from Baghdad and covered all the territories previously ruled by the Umayyad Caliphate with the exception of Andalusia and Morocco. During this period Jabir Ibn Hayyan is credited with perfecting the techniques and apparatus of distillation. Initially, the distillation of wine was confined to chemists' rudimentary laboratories. The wide spread use of distillation seems to have started much later, probably around the XIIIth century.

Christians in the East lived mainly in the Levant, with the exception of the Coptic Church that prospered in Egypt and remains to this day. The Levant was largely under the rule of the Byzantine Empire with Constantinople (modern day Istanbul) as its capital when the Prophet Mohammed started calling on the people of Hejaz in the Arab Peninsula to convert to Islam in 610 AD. Two years after the Prophet's death in 632 AD, the Rashidun Caliphs (the first four caliphs) conquered the Levant, and the region (including Lebanon) remained a

---

32 A village in the north of Lebanon

part of the Islamic world, apart from the 200 years between 1098 AD and 1291 AD when the Crusaders invaded the region. During these years, the northern and coastal areas of Greater Syria were ruled by Christians from the West whom locals called *al-Ifranj or al-Faranja* (the Franks).

In 1536, King Francis I of France and the Turkish Sultan Suleiman the Magnificent signed a strategic collaboration agreement that included placing Christian regions within the Ottoman Empire under French guardianship. In 1638, France publicly offered its protection to Catholic Christians living under Ottoman rule, including the Marontie community. In 1640, the first mission of Jesuit priests arrived in Lebanon and settled in Sidon, Tripoli, Beirut, and finally in the village of Ksara in the Bekaa. In 1860, they started cultivating grapes to make wine. To briefly describe what life was like at the time, everything revolved around monasteries and the Church. Land owners could avoid paying taxes to Turkish rulers if they placed their properties in the hands of a monastery. Even today, some small villages in Lebanon are still mostly, or entirely, owned by the Church.

Farmers were considered part of the parish, and "partners" with the monastery, who allowed them to invest in a plot of land in exchange for a share of the profits. During harvest season, the best grapes were kept for daily consumption while the sweeter grapes were used to make raisins, molasses, and vinegar to keep for the winter. At the end of the season, the remaining grapes would be gathered and placed in barrels for fermentation and, later, distillation. The grapes used to make araq are therefore the lowest in quality of each year's harvest.

The *karaki* stills that used to be available at most monasteries were operated by the partners and parishioners of the Church. The monastery looked after the equipment while the partners undertook the distillation process. Today, monasteries still produce araq alongside wine, and some have annual feasts to celebrate the season of araq production like the Deir Kfifan monastery or the St John Monastery in Khenchara (both in Mount Lebanon). The Maronite Church has 75 monasteries in Lebanon in total.

With their overall religious authority residing outside of the Middle East, Christians residing in the Levant were able to stay up-to-date with the latest industrial developments in the West and import technologies. In Greater Syria, the copper markets in Damascus, Homs, and Aleppo became the main manufacturing hubs for the *karaki* stills in the regions.

Araq in Lebanon was more than an alcoholic drink. It was part of the national identity. Christians who settled in the region's mountains considered araq a key part of their diet. The climate in these mountains was cold and harsh, and the inhabitants ate fatty and preserved foods. In some places like Mount Lebanon, people even ate raw meat because it was cheaper. In these harsh conditions, araq was favoured over other alcoholic drinks. Imported drinks were non-existent, and wine consumption was largely limited to the upper classes and the clergy.

Drinking araq was one of the core traditions Lebanese emigrants took with them. It was a reminder of the joys of home and a source of comfort on lonely nights. Wherever they went, their culinary traditions accompanied them, not least of them, araq.

Christians residing in the Middle East can be credited for the continued existence of alcoholic drinks in the region. Wherever Christians went, they took their drinks with them, and consequently, with fewer Christians living in the region, the production and consumption of alcoholic drinks has diminished.

WHO INVENTED ARAQ?

Who invented araq? Who decided to add aniseed to alcohol to produce araq? Where did it happen? When? Why?

Unfortunately, we don't have answers to these questions and are unlikely to get them any anytime soon. There are very few references, texts, books or any other historical traces to guide us in the right direction. Religious books and historical accounts only talk about alcohol or wine in general without going into details about their different type, colours and production processes.

Poets, whose writings reflect their societies and culture, described their drinks but fell short of describing them in detail. Was araq considered as a type of wine and therefore included in texts written about the latter?

From what we know, we can only come up with theories. They may resemble the truth, and might even be the truth, but lacking any documented proof, they remain nothing more than theories. At best, they are conclusions drawn from historical patterns in this part of the world where araq was born; Syria, Palestine, Jordan, Lebanon, and Iraq, or what is known as the Fertile Crescent.

The moment in history when distilled alcohol was born was probably around 800 AD when Jaber Ibn Hayyan perfected the alembic, a type of still. While the English word "alembic" derives from Arabic, in the Levant, this type of still is in fact called a karaki[33]. Before then, alcohol was produced by fermentation only, as was the case with beer and wine. However, around the IXth century, there is evidence of the distillation of wine by Arab and Persian chemists.

The consensus among scholars is that ancient Greeks did not have a word for the color "blue". It is often noted that Homer's "Iliad" and "Odyssey" do not include a single instance of the word[34]. To the most celebrated writer of Ancient Greek, the sea looked "wine-dark". In 2018, independent scholar Paul Skallas emitted a theory that disputes the status quo. His theory is anchored in knowledge of ancient Middle Eastern cultures that scholars of ancient Greece often lack. He notes that in ancient Semitic languages the word "K-H-L" referred to applying eyeliner, and by extension to the color "blue". Skallas cites biblical passages where the word "K-H-L" is used to describe the dark blue bags that appear under the

---

33 The Levantine word *karaki* is of uncertain origin, but is probably very old. It was used by al-Dimashqi (1256–1327), a medieval geographer, when describing the distillation of rosewater in Damascus. One possible origin for the word might be the classical Arabic verb qarq, an onomatopoeic, which describes the sound of water boiling. Alternatively, the Syriac noun keraka has the sense of circulation or circuit which could conceivably be used to describe an instrument of distillation. If asked about the origin of the word, a Levantine would probably answer by "God knows best"! Thank you to Professor Tarif Khalidi for suggesting a possible Arabic origin and Professor Mario Kozah (American University of Beirut) for suggesting a possible Syriac origin.

34 This was discussed by William Gladstone in his "Studies on Homer and the Homeric Age" (1858), before he became Prime Minister of Britain.

eyes after much drinking. And there lies the connection to alcohol[35]. The English term alcohol comes from the Arabic word *al-kuhool*, itself derived from the word *kohl*, a modern version of the ancient "K-H-L", designating oils and creams applied as eye makeup Was Homer's Aegean sea "wine-dark" or more simply "dark blue" like the eyeliner of his contemporary belles?

With the alembic, people were able to produce alcohol from any type of fermentable fruit, including apples, figs, grapes, dates, plums, beetroot, and so forth.

However, the alcohol they extracted was bitter, dry, and hard to swallow. It burned the throat like cold water being poured on hot metal. At first, people used it for medicinal purposes but slowly they started looking for ways to improve the taste, so they could drink it socially without grimacing in disgust. People had experienced the joy alcohol brought and they wanted more.

The period that followed the invention of the *karaki* was mainly one of trial and error, adjustments, repeated experiments, and trying out different flavours, herbs and botanicals. In the case of araq, the best plant found to flavour the distilled product was aniseed.

The addition of aniseed was probably not a coincidence like the discovery of fermentation but rather the result of different experiments to find the best flavour to add to alcohol. The product combining distilled alcohol and aniseed was araq.

---

35 Source: Paul Skallas, Medium (25 June 2018).

But why aniseed? Turning the question on its head, why use anything but aniseed? If we had to choose an ingredient today to flavour alcohol, considering all the plants and herbs available in the region, the obvious choice would still be aniseed. It is the best and sweetest botanical.

When chewed raw, aniseed gives out a pleasant fragrance and a sweet taste. Under high temperatures, the seeds maintain their consistency and do not dissolve in the alcohol. These are all excellent characteristics when looking for a tasty ingredient that will not change the consistency or colour of alcohol. This is not to say that other plants cannot be used to flavour alcohol. However, most tend to change the qualities of the liquid, and while some do not dissolve into the alcoholic liquid, they also fail to alter the taste. Aniseed, boiled with the alcohol, seems to be the perfect ingredient to achieve a better taste without affecting the consistency or any other characteristics.

WHAT IS ANISEED?
Aniseed in Alcoholic Drinks:

Most references suggest that aniseed comes from Egypt. Archaeologists found *pimpinella anisum*, the scientific name of aniseed, in tombs in the eastern desert of Thebes and the plant was mentioned in Pharaonic scripts for medical treatments.

Aniseed is an herb that grows half a meter high with a thin granulated stem and long branches divided into round pointy leaves ending in small white umbels whose flowers turn into brown fruit when mature. The plant's lifecycle lasts one year, and it grows today in southern Europe, Turkey, Iran, China, India, Japan, and in the south and east of the United States. The plant had considerable medicinal importance in ancient times, and Hippocrates recommended aniseed to clear the respiratory tract from mucus. His contemporary, Theophratus, adopted a more romantic point of view and believed that the sweet aroma of aniseed placed near a person's bed would help the sleeper have pleasant dreams. In the Maghreb, aniseed is called the "sweet seed" and in Central America, women eat aniseed to help produce milk.

Aniseed was considered an important commercial good in the Mediterranean Basin and was even used as a currency to pay taxes. It became so popular as a spice, medicine, and perfume that King Edward I of England imposed taxes on the plant to help rebuild London Bridge.

Aniseed in Alcoholic Drinks

Name	Country	Description
Aguardiente	Latin America, especially: Brazil, Columbia, Ecuador and Mexico	The name literally means burning or flaming water (Sp: *Ardiente*, burning and *agua*, water). Its alcohol content is high and can go up to 60%.
Absinthe	Switzerland	It has a high alcohol content and was popular among artists at the start of 20th century, especially in France.
Anisette	France, Italy, Portugal, Spain	A sweet tasting liqueur with an alcohol content ranging between 25% and 45%.
Pastis	France	Has a similar taste to araq and is diluted with water to become drinkable. Its alcohol content ranges between 40% and 45% and it is very popular in the south of France.
Ouzo	Greece	Similar to araq in terms of taste and characteristics. It can be consumed on its own or mixed with water.
Mastika	Romania	It is made from the mastic resin tree and is named after it.
Tagermeiter	Germany	A fragrant liqueur that aids digestion and has an alcohol content of 35%.
Sambuca	Italy	Made from aniseed oil and is available in white, blue and black. It has a high alcohol content.
Raki	Turkey, the Balkans	Turkey's national drink. Similar to araq, but with a lower alcohol content.
Chartreuse	France	Based on a mixture of plants and named after the monastery that first produced it. It has an alcohol content of 45-55%. Comes in yellow and green varieties

THE PRODUCTION OF ARAQ

- The Soil:

For every region and soil there is a vine. To know the characteristics of the soil and the climate is to know what kind of vines to plant. Calciferous soil in a dry and hot climate necessitates a specific type of vine while loamy soil rich in minerals, rocky soil, or sandy soil all require other types. Choosing the correct type of vine to suit the soil and the climate reflects on the quality and richness of the crop, and on the sweetness of the grapes.

- The Vine:

References indicate that the vine has been around as long as Man.

The Vitis Vinifera plant can survive at almost any altitude but in the context of Lebanon, the vine thrives between 600 and 1,200 meters above sea level. Below 600 meters, the climate is too warm and humid, and pollution can lead to fungal diseases, which would require chemical treatments and would therefore undermine the quality of the fruits. Above 1,200 meters, the climate becomes too cold, delaying harvest and affecting the quantity of sugar in the fruit, and consequently the alcohol percentage after fermentation.

On average, there are 200 to 250 grams of sugar in one litre of grape juice and every 16.83 grams leads to one percentage of alcohol content.

For example, if a bottle of wine is marked as having an

alcohol level of 13%, this means that for every litre of the initial grape juice, there were 218 grams of sugar (1683 x 13 = 218).

In 1870, the Phylloxera blight originating from the eastern regions of the United States hit vines across the world, with crops in Europe hit especially hard. It took 30 years before scientists were able to control it. They discovered resistant vines in the United States, took samples, and sent them to labs in Montpelier in France. There, it was revealed that the roots of the vines had helped them resist the bug. The strong roots became known as rootstocks and were adopted around the world as a basis for vines by farmers who would graft the types of vines they wanted onto the rootstocks in the spring. The basis of most vineyards nowadays is in fact rootstocks. In the end, it seems, both the problem and the solution came from the United States.

- Varieties of Grapes:

When it comes to araq, the grapes recommended are listed in order of importance below:
- Obaideh
- Miqsasi
- Maghdushi

These grapes are rich in sugar, have a sweet taste, and are planted across Lebanon and Syria. The sugar content per litre of juice ranges between 200 and 250 grams, a good rate for distillation.

- **Harvest:**

The percentage of sugar in grapes is what determines harvest time. Farmers start by checking this percentage using modern equipment like a densimeter or a refractometer to accurately identify sugar quantities over 200 grams per litre. This is the modern method. In the past, farmers would taste the grapes to assess their sweetness. With experience, they learned how the soil interacts with the vine and by tasting the grapes were able to assess the sugar content with an accuracy that almost matches that of modern equipment.

- **Yeast:**

Yeast is made up of a type of bacteria that is present all around us in the air, tree barks, fruits, soil, etc.

We do not know when, how or where yeast was first invented. Cuneiform texts found in Egypt only refer to its use in bread. Most likely, dough made from flour and water was left outside in warm weather for too long until it fermented and increased in size. After it was baked, it had likely risen more and tasted better than flat bread. And so, from then on, bread was mostly made with yeast using small pieces of the previous day's fermented bread. This continued to be the case until yeast was isolated and later added separately to the dough.

In the Old Testament, as Moses was rushing to leave Egypt, he took unfermented dough with him. This is why Jews will eat unleavened bread during Passover.

For a long time, scientists were unsure what yeast actually is. Is it a living organism made up of bacteria or is it a collection of cells that change to produce fermentation? The answer became clear in 1859 when the French scientist Louis Pasteur found that the dust around the grape is what gets fermented, that native yeast is indeed a kind of bacteria, and that live cells alone can drive fermentation.

- Fermentation:

Grapes are pressed to obtain pure grape juice free of any solids like the stalk, pips or skin, as these could affect the amount of impurities and methanol in the final product. Methanol can exacerbate the symptoms experienced after drinking, or what we know as a hangover: headaches, and dryness of the mouth and throat. These sensations can also be easily experienced after eating grapes, drinking grape juice, or chewing the pips or skin. Once the juice is pressed, it is placed in containers and yeast is added to start the fermentation process.

With the fermentation process underway, how do producers know when it is complete? Today, modern equipment can accurately read the liquid's density, sugar content, and alcohol percentage.

When the liquid reaches a density of 996 on the Gay-Lussac scale (water has a density of 1,000 on the Gay-Lussac scale), the fermentation process is complete. At this point, the liquid can either be stored in special containers to be consumed later as wine or it can be distilled to obtain ethanol. If the liquid is simply left untreated after fermentation, it becomes vinegar.

This is the optimal process to obtain good quality and healthy ethanol from grapes.

Of course, all this is a more modern process. Traditionally, Lebanese producers living in the country's mountainous regions would press the grapes along with all their solid components then leave the resulting liquid in containers for approximately 20 days to allow the natural fermentation process to take place. The liquid would then be sieved and distilled to make araq.

As we said earlier, modern equipment can pinpoint exactly when the fermentation process is complete and when the liquid is ready to be distilled. But how did producers know before these machines were invented?

A popular saying in Lebanon says, "When you can see your face reflected in the barrel, it's time to light the fire." In other words, when a person can see their face reflected in the liquid inside the container, the fermentation is done, and the liquid is ready to be distilled. This saying was once considered as the golden rule of araq making. If the fermented liquid is not distilled, it gradually turns to vinegar and any attempt to make alcohol from it results in low-quality products that can cause a very bad hangover.

- Distillation:

The *karaki* is a device made from copper and shaped like an upside-down funnel: wide at the base and narrow at the top. A spiral tube comes out of the device and leads to a container placed on the ground where the ethanol is collected drop by drop. The verb "distill" describes the act of falling in drops.

When the wine placed at the base of the *karaki* is heated, the alcohol it contains evaporates first and travels upwards through the device and then through a tube surrounded by cold water. The vapour condenses and turns into ethanol.

As for the quality of the ethanol produced from grapes, it is directly linked to the type of grape juice that was initially fermented.

Grape juice with a high percentage of sugar and no solid components produces high-quality ethanol with lower methanol levels, and vice versa.

This again leads us to the question; without modern equipment, how did people in the past know if the ethanol they extracted was of good quality and when the distillation process was complete?

Very simply, the producer would collect a sample of "fresh" ethanol (half an espresso cup) and would pour it on the bottom part of the *karaki*. He/she would then light the fire underneath and watch. If the liquid burnt quickly and the flame lasted a while, the ethanol produced was good and the distillation should continue. If the liquid either did not burn or only burnt for a few seconds, the distillation process should stop since the alcohol percentage in the liquid had become too low.

Ethanol is without doubt the most important component of araq. While it can be extracted from any type of fruit with a high percentage of sugar - like dates, figs, apples, sugarcane, etc.

- where the juice can be fermented and distilled, the Lebanese araq is based on ethanol extracted from pure grape juice only.

- **The Addition of Aniseed:**

The ethanol has a volume of 20° to 22° on the Cartier scale and should be left to rest for at least six months keeping the same alcohol volume. After six months, it is diluted in distilled water to reach a volume of 17° to 18° Cartier and placed in the *karaki* once again (after the *karaki* is cleaned to remove any residue that might affect the taste of the araq) and 2.5 kg of aniseed added for every 20 litres of liquid. The distillation process is launched for the second time at low heat, and the new liquid is collected drop by drop in the container at the end of the tube.

Another golden rule of araq making is summarized in the saying, "The flame of a lamp is enough for araq". A low stable heat is ideal for distilling the ethanol after the aniseed has been added. A strong and changeable flame can cause the content of the *karaki* to boil, and consequently the Anise seeds to break and release their oils, which would undermine the quality of the araq. Moreover, too much aniseed can also be harmful, causing the drinker to feel drowsy and experience headaches.

Twenty minutes into the second distillation process, the collected liquid is placed aside. At this point, it contains high levels of harmful methanol and is distilled for a third time to obtain good-quality, smooth and healthy araq. While all this is going on, producers constantly monitor the percentage of alcohol in the liquid.

Araq starts off with a high alcohol volume ranging between 33° and 35° Cartier, which gradually deceases to 22° Cartier as the liquid gradually turns white in colour from the addition of aniseed. The distillation process is then stopped.

Aniseed is indeed what gives araq its white colour when mixed with water. As we mentioned earlier, too much aniseed can be harmful, making you drowsy and causing a headache. Too much aniseed is evident if small crumbs appear at the surface of the liquid after adding ice cubes, these have a high content of aniseed and the araq is said to have "curdled" like milk.

At 28° to 33° of alcohol volume, araq is considered at its best and is known as *Zahra* (meaning "flower" in Arabic).

The percentage of alcohol in the produced liquid is now measured with modern and precise equipment, but in the past, producers could only rely on their senses of smell and taste to determine the quality and alcohol percentage of their araq. While their estimates could only be exactly that, estimates, their years of experience honed their skills into strong, albeit not totally accurate, measurement methods. If the alcohol content was found to be too high, more water would be added to the glass and vice versa. Their best equipment was their own noses and mouths.

Today, a type of araq that can sustain a larger quantity of water before turning white is often called "triple" or *mtallat* in Arabic. However, this is not the correct terminology. Araq can only be called *mtallat* if it has been distilled three times (i.e. a triple distillation).

First distillation: Extraction of ethanol from the fermented grape juice.

Second distillation: Aniseed is added to grape ethanol to create araq

Third distillation: A quantity of the grape ethanol produced during the first distillation and the same quantity of the araq produced in the second distillation are mixed and 1.25 kg of aniseed is added for every 20 litres. The new mixture is distilled to produce *Araq mtallat*.

The resulting product is purer, sweeter, smoother, and has lower levels of methanol. Its side effects are also milder.

After Distillation:

The araq collected from the *karaki* is rich in gas and has a sharp smell and taste. It should therefore be allowed to rest to get rid of the impurities that remained from the distillation, and to allow the taste of the aniseed to mix well with the taste of the grapes.

The best way to age araq is to place it in clay containers that allow it to breathe and releases its gases. Producers often use clay barrels and transfer the liquid from one barrel to the other (or even stir the liquid inside the same barrel) to aerate it. This action makes the araq purer and cleaner, but it does reduce its volume by approximately 3%. The araq should be kept in the barrels for at least a year to obtain a smooth taste and a unique smell of both grapes and aniseed. Once rested, the liquid is transferred to glass bottles called "*mqashasheh*". They consist of a glass balloon-shaped bottle with a long and narrow opening at the top encased in a metal basket. Straw (*qash* in Arabic) is placed between the glass and the metal for protection. Traditionally, every house would have such containers in its basement to store araq away from the sun. With every year that passes, the araq becomes smoother and better.

Once the araq is ready to be consumed, how can you tell if it it is any good? This kind of knowledge only comes with experience. By tasting different types of araq, a person learns to differentiate good araq made from pure grape juice and naturally grown aniseed from other lesser-quality products.

A person who only drinks araq once every month or two will not usually be able to tell the difference because the market is saturated with lower-grade products. Some of these products are made from different fruit to grapes and with the addition of different botanicals to aniseed. They look the same as triple distilled araq but smell and taste different. They do not smell of grape or aniseed but rather of alcohol mixed with fruit. A true "expert," however, can always tell the difference.

The Production of Araq

1. Grapes

Araq can be produced from all types of grapes but the best three are: Obaideh, Miqsasi, Maghdushi.

2. Grape juice

Pure grape juice free of any solid components.

3. Fermentation

Until the liquid reaches a density of 996 on the Gay-Lussac scale (water has a density of 1,000 on the scale).

4. Distillation

The liquid is distilled to obtain ethanol.

5. The ethanol is left to rest

The resulting ethanol is left to rest for at least six months to reach an alcohol volume ranging between 20° and 22° Cartier.

When used in the distillation, this volume should be diluted by adding water to reach 17° to 18° Cartier.

6. Distillation of the grape ethanol and addition of aniseed

At a rate of 2.5 Kg for every 20 litres to obtain regular araq.

7. Additional distillation

A quantity of regular araq (from Step 6) is added to a similar quantity of grape ethanol (from Step 5), then 1.25 kg of aniseed is added for every 20 litres of the mixture to obtain a smooth tasting *Araq mtallat* (triple distillation).

8. The araq is left to rest for one year

The araq is left to age for one year in clay containers. This allows the liquid to breathe and get rid of any impurities. It should be stirred from time to time to allow the aniseed to mix well with the liquid.

9. Ready for consumption

The araq is placed in glass bottles and stored away from direct sunlight to preserve its quality.

ALCOHOL CONTENT

In the eighteenth century, sailors were partly paid in rum (an alcoholic drink made from distilling sugarcane after fermentation). To make sure the rum was not diluted in water to increase its volume, the British government employed controllers who would melt a small quantity of gunpowder in a cup of rum. If the surface of the liquid caught fire and the flame was steady and even, they knew the rum was good. They had realized that the gunpowder only caught fire when the alcohol content in the rum reached 57.15% of the liquid. Since then, this rate was adopted as the "100 degrees proof" based on which the alcohol content of various drinks was measured across the British Empire.

The rest of Europe had a different way of measuring alcohol content and, across the Atlantic, the American continent had its own methods too. It was only in 1973 that unified standards were adopted based on the French Gay-Lussac principle, which measures the percentage that ethanol makes up of the overall liquid. The temperature of the liquid must be 20°C when performing the test. The resulting rate is referred to as "alcohol by volume" (ABV). For example, if a bottle of alcohol reads "40% vol", this means that the liquid inside the bottle is made up of 40% alcohol and 60% other material (chiefly sugar and water).

It is now rare to find in Europe drinks with an alcohol content higher than 45% ABV. Drinks with higher contents can be found illegally such as the Irish drink Poteen, which can have an alcohol content of up to 95%.

Comparison of Alcohol Volumes

Alcohol volume, international measurement unit	Alcohol volume in Araq, unit adopted in Arab countries	Notes
40%	17.5	Most legal beverages sold across the world have an alcohol content of 40% to 45% at most
45%	18.5	
50%	20	
65%	25	
72.5%	28	The alcohol content of traditional Araq only (Baladi)
77%	30	
86.5%	35	

Note: Most Arab countries have adopted the Joseph Cartier scale, while the rest of the world tends to use the Gay Lussac ABV scale, which measures the volume of ethanol compared with the overall liquid. Packages of alcoholic drinks in the Arab countries will generally display both scales, thereby allowing the consumer to understand the alcohol content of the beverages. The table above provides an example of the international scale and its equivalent in the Arab world. To measure Araq's approximate alcohol content according to the ABV scale, the Joseph Cartier unit should be multiplied by approximately 2.5.

Araq Compared with Other Alcoholic Drinks

Type of drink	Alcohol volume for homemade products	Alcohol volume legally approved for sale
Beer	2%-12%	4%-6%
Vodka	35%-50%	40%
Whisky	40%-55%	40%-43%
Araq Baladi made from grapes (traditional araq)	72%-83%	45%-60%
Araq made from grapes	72%-83%	45%-60%
Araq	40%-55%	40%-45%
Poteen	60%-95%	45%

Note: In most parts of the world, it is illegal to sell any alcoholic beverage with an alcohol content exceeding 45%.

Alcohol in Lebanon

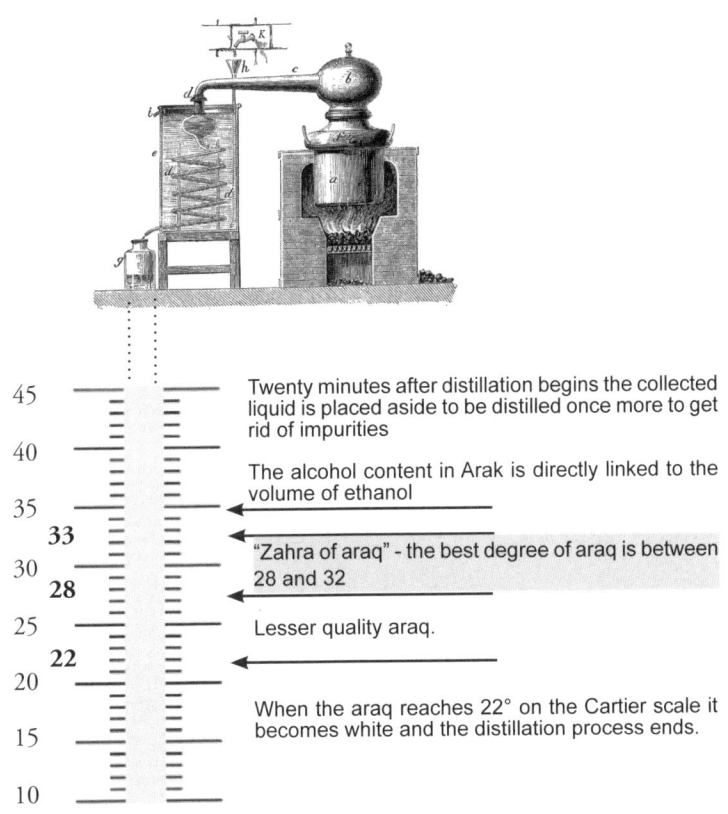

45 —
40 —
35 —
  33
30 —
  28
25 —
  22
20 —
15 —
10 —

Twenty minutes after distillation begins the collected liquid is placed aside to be distilled once more to get rid of impurities

The alcohol content in Arak is directly linked to the volume of ethanol

"Zahra of araq" - the best degree of araq is between 28 and 32

Lesser quality araq.

When the araq reaches 22° on the Cartier scale it becomes white and the distillation process ends.

ARAQ AND THE LAW

On 7 June 1937, a law was published in Lebanon's Official Gazette regulating the production of araq in the country. In its first article, the law stipulated that only drinks made from the fermentation of grapes and later their distillation with Anise can be called araq. Its second article defined drinks called araq but made from other substances as false goods.

Alcohol in general, and araq in particular, was very popular at the start of the 20th century, leading Lebanon's military authorities to issue a decision limiting the times when alcohol could be sold. According to this decision, alcohol could only be sold between noon and 2 pm and then between 6 pm and 9 pm. Bars and distilleries had to close at 10 pm and violations were met with harsh punishment.

The same newspaper published an article on 16 October 1920 referencing a sentence issued against a Mr. Salim al-Hashim for a fine of two Liras for selling alcohol to soldiers.

Today, araq is legally produced in Lebanon in three kinds, regulated by the Lebanese Standards Institution (LIBNOR).

Indonesian Araq

A drink called Arak can be found on the Indonesian island of Bali. Although it shares the same name as the araq produced in Arab countries, the two drinks are completely different. The Indonesian Arak is produced by distilling fermented sweet wine extracted from coconut flowers or rice dough mixed with coconut milk. Its alcohol content is high, and it is often used in medicine and in religious celebrations.

Sri Lankan Arrack

In Sri Lanka, a drink known as arrack is widely consumed, produced from fermented and distilled coconut tree sap. It is the island's national drink. While unlike the Lebanese or Indonesian araq, like both, the origin of the name is Arabic.

Counterfeit Araq

Cheating in araq production is not just a matter of using different ingredients to grapes and aniseed. Some araqs are even made without distillation by simply mixing aniseed essence with any type of artificial ethanol. The resulting product looks exactly like triply distilled araq but smells and tastes more like liquorice. This type of counterfeit araq is dangerous. Not only are its side effects more acute (headaches, pain around the eyes, dry throat), but it can also cause blindness if consumed regularly. It is often found in some markets outside Lebanon and Syria. Unfortunately, tourists and foreigners curious about the drink sometimes fall prey to it since they have no way of knowing that it is not genuine Lebanese araq.

Key Characteristics and Standards Set by LIBNOR[1]

Name	Characteristics
Araq Baladi made from grapes	An alcoholic drink produced exclusively from the fermentation of grapes suitable for araq production. It is distilled three times with aniseed seeds using a traditional *karaki* at a temperature no higher than 86°C. It is aged for six months.
Araq made from grapes	An alcoholic drink produced from the fermentation of grapes suitable for araq production. It is distilled with aniseed seeds or aniseed oil.
Araq	An alcoholic drink produced using one of the below methods: 1. Using ethanol mixed or redistilled with natural flavours and fragrant oils. 2. Using ethanol redistilled with aniseed seeds or herbs with a similar taste. 3. Using a combination of methods 1 and 2. 4. Mixing the results of methods 1, 2 and 3 with araq made from grapes.

Note: In most parts of the world, it is illegal to sell any alcoholic beverage with an alcohol content exceeding 45%.

---

1   Lebanese Standards Institution

Alcohol in Lebanon

Alcohol Content	Comments
45%-60%	This applies to traditional *araq baladi* produced using traditional methods. Its production cost is high and is usually only made at private homes. Is it produced by some Lebanese companies for commercial use with an alcohol content below or equal to 45%. The best grapes for its production are: Obaideh, Miqsasi and Maghdushi.
40%-45%	Most commercial araqs fall within this category. They are alcoholic drinks made from crops other than grapes. The liquid is distilled with natural flavours and fragrances such as aniseed oil, liquorice, mastic, fennel, etc. It is widely available in the market.
40%-45%	Most commercial araqs fall within this category. They are alcoholic drinks made from crops other than grapes. The liquid is distilled with natural flavours and fragrances such as aniseed oil, liquorice, mastic, fennel, etc. It is widely available in the market.

ARAQ AND THE COMMUNITY

Rapid industrial advances following the Second World War radically changed people's daily lives and customs across the Arab World, especially in the Fertile Crescent. However, while this change did help improve quality of life, it has not always proven beneficial. Adopted without proper evaluation and study, these advances sometimes led to chaos and devastation. Industrial developments were linked to a notion of "civilisation" that slowly took over at the expense of people's environment and social customs. People living at the time of these changes in the region would have found themselves caught in the middle: searching for happiness in a "civilised" society but never truly fitting in and longing for an authentic community that was left far behind. There was no going back. When we talk about araq in the community, we are usually talking about the period before modern industrial advances. Lebanon has been affected by these changes more than some other countries in the region because, in addition to adopting more open policies, at the same time, it had to deal with the wave of petrodollars that arrived from the Arab Gulf. Long-held traditions were shaken and gradually lost as the country was set on a path towards a false "civilisation." Indeed, these very same traditions were often portrayed as an obstacle to modernity while in reality, civilisation without authenticity is meaningless and an empty shell.

A self-sufficient farmer is a sultan in disguise

It is said that the Emir Bashir II (1767-1850), one of Lebanon's most famous royal historical figures, was once hosted by a peasant for three days, as the traditions of Arab hospitality dictate. At the end of the visit, the Emir thanked the farmer for his hospitality. The latter replied that there was no need as all the food and drink provided was part of the house's winter provisions. Nothing new had been bought. Impressed, the prince said: "A self-sufficient farmer is a sultan in disguise".

These words are now famous and perfectly describe what life was like in Lebanon's mountains, where provisions collected for the harsh autumn and winter transformed a simple peasant into a sultan. Grains formed the biggest part of these provisions, especially wheat that was milled weekly to make wholemeal bread. Homes were also often equipped with specialized ovens to supply the family with the bread they needed.

Jams and preserves were another staple in the pantry. They were usually offered to guests who spent the evening chatting and socialising as gas lamps lit the room (Lebanon's electricity company EDL wasn't established until 1964) alongside dried figs, walnuts, raisins and a glass of sweet wine or sweet liqueur made from berries, apricots or plums.

Other staples included the protein-rich *Kishk*, a powdery cereal of burghul, and *Qawarma*, preserved mincemeat used as a substitute for fresh meat, which was rare and only available on holidays and special occasions.

However, the one thing every home considered an essential- and versatile - commodity was araq. The bad batches were used for cleaning the house, to disinfect wounds, to remedy stomach aches, and to calm nerves. The good batches were kept for special occasions, whether happy or sad. Family gatherings would not start before the most senior member raised his glass and the clinging sound announced the beginning of the feast. The sound of this opening bell would be followed by many more and by happy cheers during happy occasions or silent patience during sad ones.

The sounds of the mountain are often still and quiet. But when people raise their glass and give freedom to their emotions, this silence is disrupted with an explosion of happiness. Life and beauty in the mountains are not complete without araq, a fact people know and appreciate. Their respect for the vine is beautifully summarized in the words of the Lebanese poet Michel Trad who said:

> *Close the window*
> *Lest someone steal the songs we sing*
> *And blow gently on the fire*
> *The wood that burns*
> *Is the wood of our beloved vines*

Mezze and Araq

National dishes evolve spontaneously over time as people interact with the land and harvest its crops. Nature, in the end, is what dictates what food people in a certain environment and a certain community eat. The *Mezze* was born with araq, and flourished as the drink flourished.

The araq-centred *Mezze* is a unique thing. Every cuisine is rich in varied and delicious dishes. But very rarely is a sample of all the dishes made for one meal to be eaten by two people. To be clear, this is not a buffet like many hotels and restaurants offer nowadays, but rather a different and authentic experience revolving around one drink - araq.

The word *Mezze* comes from the Farsi word *Mazidan*, meaning "to taste". It is essentially a collection of small dishes served in small quantities on small plates commonly called a *sehfiye*. Vegetables and grains are considered as the first course while the second course is usually made up of a smaller collection of raw meats and *Kibbe* (a traditional dish made from meat and bulgur). The third course is reserved for warm dishes and grilled meat while dessert is often traditional sweets and fruit. Coffee is then served, marking the end of the meal.

In the middle of the 20th century, restaurants often competed with each other to serve the highest number of *Mezze* dishes in the country, with some serving over 100 varieties stacked on top of each other and tables looking more like colourful pottery displays.

An important note to make in this context is that araq is not served like a cocktail that a person can hold as he/she goes around the room and eats some peanuts. You cannot stand at the bar and ask for a shot of araq like you would a vodka. Just like other drinks, araq comes with its own culture. Wine glasses are wide at the top to give the drinker the best opportunity to smell the different bouquets. A vodka glass is small so that the content can be drunk quickly with minimal exposure to its strong aroma. A glass made for araq sits somewhere in between.

It is common knowledge that the blood running in our veins, nourishing every cell in our body, is purified in the liver. The liver is also the body's battery that supplies it with energy and power when needed and as needed. If the liver fails, the body suffers from exhaustion. If a person drinks alcohol on an empty stomach, the alcohol rushes to the blood and then to the liver to be purified. If the volume of alcohol in someone's blood is too high for the liver to handle, the body starts showing signs of relaxation since the liver is too busy purifying the blood to generate the energy the body needs. Traditional *Araq Baladi* has twice the alcohol content of whisky and should never be consumed without protein rich food. The slower a person eats and drinks, the better the liver can cope and the lower a person's chances of getting intoxicated.

This is why *Mezze* was created. When people gather around

a glass of araq, they intend to stay for hours. Therefore, they need food... and different types of food to keep them from getting bored with the same taste. Their eyes need to see different colours and their taste buds need to be delighted again and again, making the whole experience even richer and more fulfilling.

Holidays in the Mountains

The public space where villagers meet is the village square, which is often the square in front of the church or monastery in Christian villages. Gatherings on Sundays and holidays broke the routine of living in the mountains, especially in winter. On special occasions, these squares would become open air theatres where life plays out. Lovers meet in the square, disputes are settled, and the general mood of the village can be felt. If the square is empty, the village elders know that something is wrong, and they need to act while a busy square reflects a happy and harmonious community. Joys and sorrows are played out in this eternal theatre. New heroes are born every day, new stories are told, and love and hate alternate in a perfect and natural balance.

On holidays and special occasions, people would flock to the square early, some hoping to get a secret smile from a loved one and others wanting to flaunt their new clothes or hats (at a time when most people dressed more or less the same). Men would display their bravado by lifting heavy stone mortars, levers or rollers as the crowd admiring their skills grows larger and larger, and the applause and cheers grow louder and louder. Soon after, the music starts and people begin to sing. Enthusiastic young men line up shoulder to shoulder like the links of a chain, and the earth moves under their feet as they dance. The strongest among them, called Sheikh al-Shabab (loosely translated, Top Lad), holds a white handkerchief that he waves around as he separates himself from the chain and shows off his light footedness and quick movements in the centre. This is the traditional dance known as *Debke*. As they move, a person holding a small bottle of *Araq Baladi* makes his round placing the bottle on each dancer's mouth for a few seconds. Having drunk this elixir, the dancers challenge each other to intensify their steps as the sound of their stomping feet grows more aggressive and the earth seems like it is about to open.

Sheikh al-Shabab is a title every man in the village dreams of holding. It is not easy to gain, and the conditions are very strict. The man named Sheikh al-Shabab must be honourable, generous, and have a spotless reputation. He calls the araq gatherings and directs them toward the fiery events they become. The title often replaces the person's given name.

With daylight fading, the square begins to empty out slowly and people head toward their own neighbourhoods where the party is set to continue indoors at someone's house. They take advantage of the occasion to eat and drink in excess. At night, they hurry to reserve a place at the *Zajal* party concluding the day's festivities. *Zajal* is the Arabic name for popular extemporised poetry and a *Zajal* party is yet another opportunity to compete. Two or three poets – some from neighbouring villages – gather and are accompanied by the village choir. They sit on one side or a rectangular table covered with delicious food and, of course, glasses of araq. The drink loosens their tongues and releases their creativity. The poems usually start with praise and laud for the people, the place, the women, and the organisers. To show their incredible command of poetry, they ask the audience to pick a subject. Suggestions like "night and day" or "the sun and the moon" pour in, and the poets and their audience choose their sides. The improvisation starts, and the poets try their best to move their audience emotionally and physically. The dancing begins, and the tables tremble while the poets recite their verses at full volume as if forcefully implanting their words in their opponents' ears. Examples of *Zajal* are:

> *Each step of*
> *your horse*
> *as it treads,*
> *crushes the*
> *pavements of*
> *paradise*

or

> *God has set up a*
> *chair for me to rest*
> *between your breasts*

The sweetest poetry is often the least sincere... this saying was surely inspired by a *Zajal* party.

The Milk of Lions

When a family gathers around Mezze and araq, it is not unknown to see a breastfeeding mother pull her baby away from her and place a finger she has dipped in araq in its mouth. She leaves her finger for a few seconds then continues to breastfeed the child. She does this with different types of food as well, to get the baby used to the taste very early on. "The Milk of Lions" is a name given to araq that likely derives from this tradition. To be able to drink araq with the same appetite as a feeding baby is something only a man with excellent health can do, a man who is said to "have drank sufficiently of his mother's milk". No man can be truly proud in the mountains unless he can hold his araq. In fact, alongside politics and family gossip, stories are told during araq gatherings of brave men who could drink heroic amounts of araq. The stories are told with a certain amount exaggeration if they are true and with modesty if they are not. The quality of the araq is rarely a subject of conversation- because that is a given - but the number of glasses a person can drink is often up for debate. Some boast about how much they can drink, others question that number, and arguments erupt as each side tries to prove to the others they're right. Results are seldom reached, and the subject is soon changed to the walk home that will feel like hours rather than minutes, and to trying (but failing) to call your children by their correct names. The poet Elia Abu Chedid described this scene:

How can I possibly make it home drunk?
The road keeps turning
And my feet seem frozen in their place

Consensus is often reached about the quality and quantity of the food but the same cannot be said for the quantity of araq a person can claim to drink.

Araq enthusiast Elie Touma's memoir about life in the town of Deir al-Qamar[36] recounts several anecdotes. In one of them, it is said a man called Khater Tabet who lived in the village in the 19th century was known for his ability to hold his drink. When it came to araq, he had no competition, even at the age of 70. He was once invited to a wedding in the town centre. As his field was located at the bottom of the village, he had to walk uphill under the scorching sun. When he arrived, he asked for some water and was given a jug. After drinking the entire liquid in it, he asked why the water tasted of araq. Knowing his reputation as a fierce araq drinker, some of the men in the village had substituted the water in the jug with araq... about one litre of it.

Araq gatherings often start but never end, or rather rarely end on the same day. In the same memoir, Elie Touma recounts a

---

36 A village in Lebanon that used to be the capital of the Emirate of Mount Lebanon during the Ottoman period.

story from the mid-twentieth century. Bechara al-Bustani was famous in Deir al-Qamar for his ability to drink araq. The sons of Jerjes Lahoud had the same reputation in the village of Baabdat. The latter invited al-Bustani for an araq gathering on the banks of al-Iraar river near the village of Baabdat. They started drinking at 8:00 am and around noon each of the four Lahoud brothers began to withdraw from the competition one after the other. Only the youngest of the Lahouds, the former MP and minister Emile Lahoud, was left to defend the family's honour. The competition ended at 9 pm, and Lahoud said: "Yes, I did stay until the end, but I had to excuse myself several times to go to the bathroom. He stayed in his place the entire day. I am no match for him."

Emile Jerjis Lahoud (1899-1954) was not only a brilliant lawyer, MP and minister, he was also one of Lebanon's funniest poets:

> *These three sucked my blood,*
> *Sucked my blood without concern,*
> *Drinking cup [of araq], "sold" cup*[37]*,*
> *And unfinished cup!*

---

37 "Sold" is an expression used by Lebanese poker players. It is the equivalent of "all-in".

(Above) A 19th century illustration of the Lebanese mountains, complete with iconic cedar trees.

(Left) Statue of the god Baal in Latakia, Syria.

(Below) King Francis I of France (left) with the Turkish Sultan Suleiman the Magnificent, 1536.

The Milk of Lions - A History of Alcohol in the Middle East

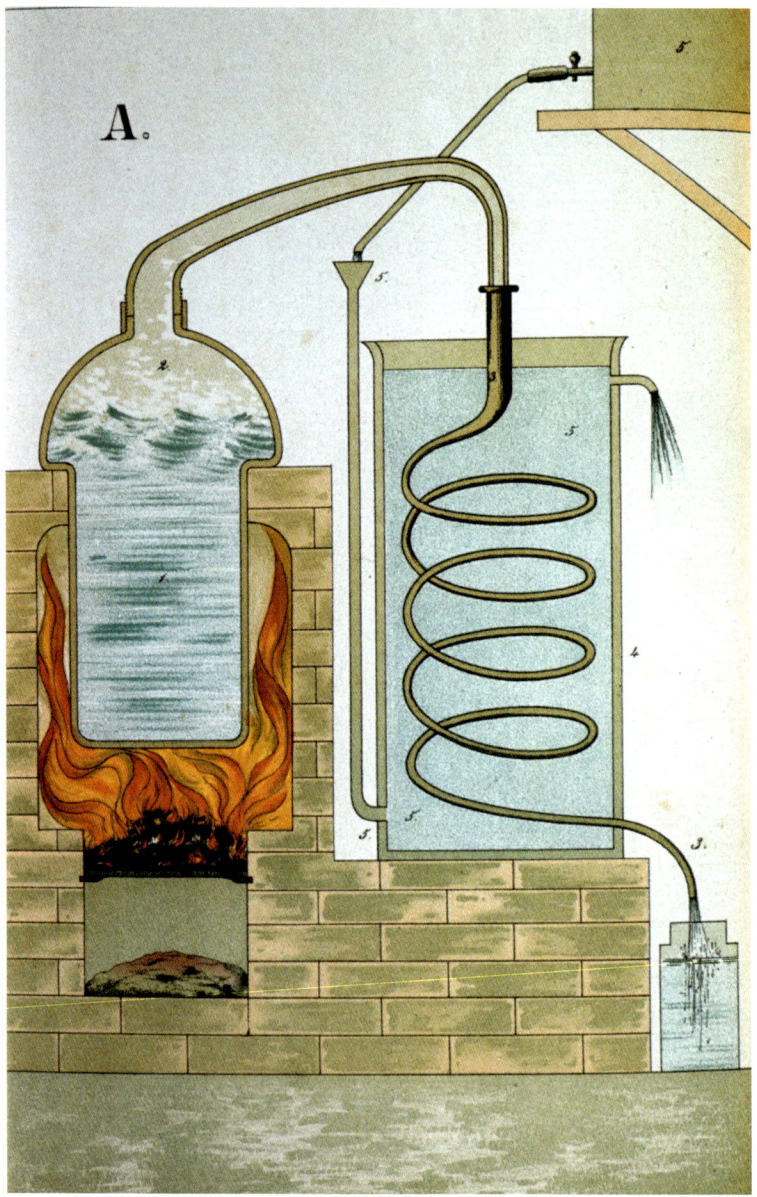

(Above) A modern *karaki* made for home use.

(Left) Mature Anise seeds

(Opposite) Operation of the *karaki* or the Alembic: the material to be distilled is placed in the container at the left side of the image. When the liquid boils, steam goes through the spiral tube immersed in cold water. This causes the steam to condense and turn into an alcoholic liquid that gathers in the container at the lower right side of the image.

The Milk of Lions - A History of Alcohol in the Middle East

(Above) Jabir Ibn Hayyan, polymath scholar who lived between the 8th and 9th centuries and is credited with having perfected the techniques and apparatus of distillation. *(Left)* Anisetta Evangelisti (also known as The Monkey) - a well known lithograph by Carlo Biscaretti dating to 1925.

(Above) Vineyards ranged across the steep slopes of the mountains that line the Bekaa valley, in Lebanon.
(Left) Harvested grapes being sorted and separated.

(Left) The old square in Deir al-Qamar, Lebanon, a typical mountain village.

The Milk of Lions - A History of Alcohol in the Middle East

(Above) A basic *karaki* following traditional design.

(Below left) A modern machine used to obtain pure grape juice. Grapes are placed in a cylinder with sieves to press the juice, as opposed to traditional design shown on facing page.

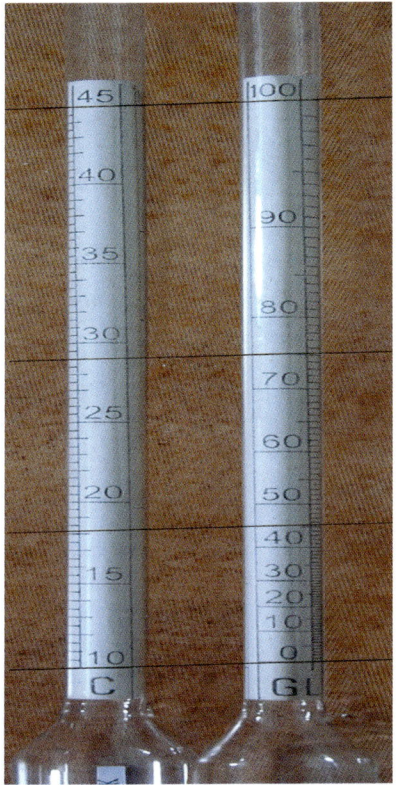

(Above) A traditional grape press

*(**Left**)* Comparison between two measurement units of alcohol content. On the right, the international ABV or Guy-Lussac scale, on the left, the Joseph Cartier Scale, popular in Arab countries.

*(**Below**)* Pottery Barrels used to age araq

The Milk of Lions - A History of Alcohol in the Middle East

(Above) 16th century English sailors. A harsh life at sea was eased by large amounts of rum.

Alcohol in Lebanon

Araq Drinking Buddies

There are three stages of inebriation in Arabic: *nashwan* (tipsy), *thamil* (intoxicated) and *sakran* (completely drunk). *Al-Sariih* is the word used to describe a person who was "knocked down" by alcohol. *Al-Irbid* is a person who harms a friend under the influence of alcohol. The Arabs used to call the stage of drunkenness "Leila" before the name became a popular girl's name. An alcohol "scholar" is a person who can achieve a state of ecstasy through alcohol without getting drunk. Conversations had in such a state of ecstasy remain with a person their whole life.

The araq "gang" doesn't form out of the blue. It is born out of years of experience and friendship. The members were chosen by fate and their relationships are nourished by araq. It is a closed group whose members are all founding members, each with his own nickname that he prefers to his own name. This nickname is chosen for him and reflects the person's behaviour or attitude toward life: the old man, the mayor, the chief, the pope, the teacher, the comrade, etc.

A member is just as proud of his nickname as he is of the stories his companions and relatives tell of his courage and strength during long nights of araq drinking, and the amounts of araq he managed to drink in one sitting. It is almost blasphemous for anyone to question the authenticity of these stories. Each member has his own field of expertise in preparing the food for the gathering; vegetables, meats, snacks, etc. The group works in harmony and silence like a theatre group rehearsing backstage waiting for the curtain to rise.

During these preparations, respect of the seasons is essential. All the food prepared must be seasonal and gatherings often celebrate the end or the start of a season. For example, snails and game birds are accompanied by green beans and pistachios. But what about the days within the season? Themes like the start of spring or summer are made up according to the weather as an excuse for celebration, and perhaps as a wish for the season to change. The group's creativity knows no end.

Like every gang, the araq gang has its leader to whom everyone remains loyal. The leader is in charge of inspiring the group and guiding its political and social stances. He is glorified and revered, and any story about him is met with complete attention as if it were a story from the Bible. This intellectual isolation, however, means that anyone who does not agree with the leader is often ignored and rejected. There is no compromise when it comes to this matter, and villages are often divided along these lines. The gang's official meeting place is called "the embassy", not out of respect for diplomacy since their opinions are not up for debate, but rather because the embassy doors remain open for friends and family to visit. One day a week is also reserved for unscheduled visits, whether short or lasting through the night, depending on the person and their agreeability. Calm discussions turn loud and noisy by the end of the evening, and reasonable arguments are mixed with emotions. It seems possible to move mountains. The Lebanese poet Michel Trad described these gatherings;

Alcohol in Lebanon

*O world,
Raise your glass
With mine*

Everyone is happy, and the world is a friendly place. At the time of writing this book, the tradition of keeping an araq "gang" remains alive and a great example of the strong friendships formed over a glass of araq among the residents of every town.

Sayings and Proverbs Related to Alcohol

Wine today... serious matters tomorrow
One of the most famous sayings dating back to the Jahiliyya period. It's said when a person is happy but receives bad news and wants to delay making any decision.

Even Malik didn't say that
Imam Malik Ibn Anas was a Muslim scholar and the founder of the Maliki rite. He was strongly opposed to alcohol and talked about it very negatively. This saying is used when describing a person who wants to criticize and insult another excessively.

Neither wine nor vinegar
Is said of someone who is indecisive and is never happy.

He sold his vineyard to buy a wine press
Is used to describe irrational behaviour, like a person who cuts down a tree to get the fruit or kills a chicken to get the eggs.

Ages like good wine
A person gets wiser with age.

Gets drunk on a raisin
Is said of a person who is quick to react and gets emotional over the smallest things.

Wait for the grapes to ripen and you can have the molasses
Patience is rewarded.

Leave the sour grapes and wait for them to ripen
Patience is rewarded.

You can share a glass with him/her
A person who is nice and good company.

If you want to get drunk, you don't count the glasses
If a person is looking for happiness, they shouldn't ask at what price it comes.

Get rid of the vineyard keepers and the money will come
The implication is that keepers tend to steal grapes from the vineyard. This saying is used when the problem lies with the people you have put in charge of something on your behalf.

The high bunch is rarely ripe
A person who wants something unattainable and therefore criticizes it. This is the same as the phrase 'sour grapes' in

English (from Aesop's fable about the fox who, unable to reach the high grapes on the vine, declared they were sour and he didn't want them anyway).

A dangling bunch is laden with unripe grapes
Similar to the previous saying.

The stupor is gone, and the ideas are back
Is said of a person who realizes they've acted irrationally and impulsively.

A vineyard by the side of the road
Is said of riches left unattended.

In with the wine, out with the secrets
This saying describes how wine helps loosen the tongue and speak the truth. i.e. *in vino veritas*.

The last grape in the bunch is pure sugar
It describes the youngest in the family who is often the most spoiled.

The sweeter the grapes the stronger the wine
Alcohol is derived from sugar. The riper the grapes, the more alcohol is produced at the end.

The first glass is a remedy, the second is joy, and the third is a waste
This saying encourages moderation in drinking.

A glass of wine a day keeps the doctor away
A widely accepted French saying.

After St Elias day, the grapes are ready
St Elias day is celebrated on July 20th and it is accepted that as of this date, the first grapes are ready to harvest in the mountains.

When August comes, harvest the grapes without worry
Most grapes ripen in August in the mountains.

Water to grow the grapes and figs
From the start of August until the middle of September, the mountains are covered by fog, and heavy dew can be seen on the leaves of vines and fig trees. The humidity is said to be essential for the fruit to ripen.

On the Assumption, grapes decorate the table
Assumption Day (the feast of the Virgin Mary) is celebrated on August 15th and tables at the celebration are often decorated with grapes in the mountains.

On August 20th, visit the vineyard without worry
Most grape varieties are said to become ripe by August 20th.

When October starts, the grapes and figs disappear
Harvest season is usually between October and November.

The sweeter the grape, the better the wine

Higher sugar content in the grapes leads to stronger wine.
The sweeter the seeds, the better the wine
Similar to the previous saying

When you can see your face reflected in the barrel, it's time to light the fire.
Grapes are placed in a container. When an araq producer can see his/her face reflected in the liquid inside the container, the fermentation is done, and the liquid is ready to be distilled.

The flame of a lamp is enough for araq
Araq should be distilled in the *karaki* over a low and steady heat.

Without drinking, the world would be chaos
Alcohol is necessary as it brings people joy and happiness.

If you know how to drink, you know how to love, and if you know how to love, you know how to drink
A French saying.

Glossary

Alcohol (Ethanol) is a volatile flammable liquid with a bitter taste. It has a lower density than water and can be mixed with water in various proportions. It is the key ingredient found in alcoholic drinks, whether fermented or distilled, and can be extracted from fruit (grapes, dates, raisins, apples, pears), grains (wheat, barley, corn), honey, starch, sugar, potato, or beetroot.

Spirits: The name given to distilled drinks with a high percentage of alcoholl, such as whisky, araq, vodka, etc., whether made from fruit or from grain.

Alcohol was probably first made using the brewing process. For instance, an analysis of antique pottery found in the north of China has revealed preserved deposits of fermented drinks made from rice, honey and fruit. These date back to the same period in history when beer production began in the East.

In 800 AD, Muslim scientist Jabir bin Hayyan is credited with perfectng the alembic distiller, (commonly known in

Lebanon as the karaki), and is believed to have distilled alcohol successfully.

Throughout history, spirits were widely consumed during daily meals, or were used for hygienic or medical purposes considering their sedative effect, or, as with Judaism and Christianity, for their religious symbolism.

Wine is known under two names in Arabic. The first, *khamr*, refers to the drink which results from the fermentation of grapes. It should be noted that the Arabic term can designate grapes as a fruit without fermentation as shown in Surat Yusuf in the Qur'an: "Indeed, I have seen myself [in a dream] pressing grapes." The word used in the Arabic text is *khamr* and, in this context, indicates grapes as a fruit.

The second name used for wine in Arabic is *nabith*. This term reflects the production process and indicates the transfer of an item (the verb nabatha in Arabic means "to dispose of"): the traditional winemaking process includes the transfer of dates, raisins or grapes in a water filled container, after which the mixture is left to react until it becomes alcoholic.

Bibliography

NOTE
Quotations from the Jewish and Christian scriptures are taken from the King James Bible (KJB). Quotations from the Qur'an are from *The Qur'an*, a translation by Tarif Khalidi (Penguin Classics, 2008). Tarif is a friend of the author who gave valuable guidance for the writing of this book.

Listed below are the principal works referred to in this book. In many instances, the works were published in Arabic and never translated in English. For these, we have transcribed the titles on a phonetic basis, as well as providing a rough translation of the title in brackets.

AHMAD SADEQ, Rajaa, *Alcohol during the Umayyad Caliphate* (Arab Diffusion Company, 2009)

AL-BUSTANI, Butrus, *Udaba al-'arab*, ("Arab Authors") (Maroun Abboud Press, 1979)

AL-MUQRI, Ali, *Wine and Alcohol in Islam* (Riyadh

al-Rayyis Press, 2007)

AL-QAYRAWANI, Abu Ishaq, *Qutb al-Surur fi Awsaf al Anabith wal-Khumur (The Pinnacle of Happiness in Describing Wines and Alcohol)*, edited by Dr. Sara Barbouchi-Ben Yahya (Al-Jamal Press, 2010)

ARVON, Henri, *Buddhism* (al-Manshurat al-Arabiya, 1985)

BOUSTANY, Fouad Ephrem, *Al-Rawaeh, ("The Masterpieces")* (Jubilé d'or, 1977)

EL-DORRY, Menna, *Wine Making in Ancient Egypt*, (from the website: www.arabworldbooks.com)

ESFAHANI, Abi Faraj, *Al-Diyarat ("Monastries")*, edited by Jalil Al-Attyeh (Riyadh al-Rayyis Press, 1991)

FARRUKH, Umar, *Al-Manhaj fi al-Adab al-Arabi,("A Primer in Arabic Literature")*

FREIHA, Anis, *Epics and Legends* (American University of Beirut Centennial Publications,1966)

GIBRAN, Kahlil, *The Prophet* (Penguin Classics, 2002)

ISKANDAR, Amjad, *Emile Lahoud, Lil-kalimah Lil-wa'an, (Emile Lahoud: "For the word, for the homeland")* (Joseph D. Raidy Press, 1966)

KAZAN, Rudyard, *L'arak et la distillerie Boutros Kazan & Fils de Beyrouth durant le mandat français* (Chronos, issue number 10, 2004, pp. 69-93)

KHALIF, Yussef (Dr.), *Hayat al-she'ar fi al-Koufa,("Poetry in Kufa")* (Supreme Council of Culture – Cairo, 1995)

KHALIL JEHA, Michel (Dr.), *Great Popular Lebanese Poets* (Dar al-'Awda, Dar al-Thaqafa, 2003)

KHAYYAM, Omar, *Rubaiyat*, Translated by Edward Fitzgerald (Forgotten Books, 2018)

KHOURY HARB, Antoine, *Lebanon, the Name and the Entity over 4,000 years* (Lebanese Heritage Foundation, 2003)

MOURANI, César (Père), *L'Architecture Religieuse de Cobiath sous les Croisés* (from the website: www.kobayat.org)

NASSIF, Emile, *Collection of Literature on Spirits and Gatherings around them* (al-Jil, 1993)

NICHOLSON, Reynold A., *Translations of Eastern Poetry and Prose* (Cambridge at the University Press, 1922)

PIERI, Dominique, *Le commerce du vin à l'époque Byzantine (IV-VII siècles)*, (Institut Français d'Archéologie du Proche-Orient, 2005)

SALIBI, Kamal, *A House of Many Mansions* (Nawfal Press, 1988)

SAMADI NAAMAN, Hana, *Les proverbes de ma mère* (Geuthner, 2010)